MY INBOX
—UNCENSORED!

Other books by Derrick Arnott

Social Domestic & Pleasure

Accidental Millionaire

Politics versus the People

MY INBOX —UNCENSORED!

**In defence of the dirty joke
and free speech:
"an eclectic compilation of comical,
candid, controversial emails from my
Inbox 2009—2019."**

Derrick Arnott

MY INBOX—UNCENSORED!

Published by Diadem Books

For information, please contact:

Diadem Books
8 South Green Drive
Airth
Falkirk
FK2 8JP
Scotland UK

www.diadembooks.com

ISBN: 978-0-244-53138-6

ACKNOWLEDGEMENTS

To the many, many contributors

from all over the world,

this is your book.

You know who you are!

Evie's tale—with a twist—will warm the coldest heart and brighten the darkest mood.

This lovely story is based on what is claimed to be a true(ish) account of a bond formed between a little girl and a group of building workers.

A young family moved onto a new estate whilst it was under construction. Work was still in progress with the plot next door. Evie, the family's five-year-old daughter, was naturally curious and spent ages hanging around and taking an interest in the activities.

Evie and the friendly gang of building workers quickly formed a bond. She was invited onto the site to share their tea breaks and chat to them.
The gang sort of adopted Evie as their project mascot and they gave her little jobs to do to make her feel important. They gave

her one of their hard hats and some gloves. She became part of the gang. She was buzzing.

After a couple of weeks the gang, with hearts of gold, had a whip round and presented Evie with an envelope containing two pounds in coins—her wages for the jobs she had done.

She took her "wages" home and proudly showed her mother. Mum thanked the workers profusely.

Next day she suggested to Evie that they should take the money to the bank and open a savings account. Evie was thrilled and this made her feel even more important.

At the bank the female cashier was tickled pink as she listened to the little girl's story—how she worked on a building site and how she got a pay packet.

"You must have worked very hard to get all this money," said the cashier.

"Yes," replied the little girl proudly. "I worked every day with Steve, Wayne and Mike. We're building a big house."

"My goodness gracious!" said the cashier. "And will you be working on the big house next week too?"

Evie thought for a moment. Then said seriously:

"I think so. Provided those wankers from Jewsons deliver the fucking bricks on time."

ABOUT THIS BOOK

If the swear words used in this story offended you, then read no further. If you chuckled, then perhaps you may be broad minded enough to recognise that swearing can enhance the impact of some stories and jokes.

Evie's tale is one of many circulated by email before the advent of more sophisticated types of social media and at a time when PC, the threat to free speech and to our sense of humour in Britain, were at their most intense.

Thankfully, the consequences of this folly were exposed by the attempts to cover up the sex abuse scandals in towns and cities throughout the country for fear of upsetting some groups of people.

Emails provided a degree of anonymity behind which people could avoid arrest by expressing their opinions—and, if you like, their prejudices.

The compiler makes no excuse for including in this book a few "f" words, "c" words and other things which some might find offensive. Don't blame him. He didn't send them—and he does not necessarily agree with them. But he defends the right for them to be expressed.

Nor does he regret including some emails which may disturb the sensitivities of some people who take their religions (and other things) too seriously. He is sorry if they do so, but hopes that these people may learn to recognise that their behaviour and perceived idiosyncrasies may seem odd, amusing and sometimes unacceptable to others not familiar with their cultures—and to accept this.

Only when we all begin to recognise this.
Only when we can accept that others may find our differences a source of amusement.
Only when we understand that poking light hearted fun at our differences does not constitute hatred.
Only then will meaningful integration and peaceful co-existence become possible.

The Public Order and Racial and Religious Hatred Acts sought, so far with only a modicum of success, to achieve these objectives. These are some of the extracts from these Acts and their guidelines:

"...in a free, democratic and tolerant society, people are able to robustly exchange views, even when these views may cause offence."

"To secure a conviction (under the Acts) it must be proved that it was the intention of the defendant to stir up hatred.... and that his or her actions were motivated by this intention."

As the French philosopher Voltaire so rightly observed:
"I may not agree with what you say—but I will defend to the death your right to say it."

If only those PC zealots who would seek to control the way we must think, shared Voltaire's philosophy and his wisdom.

When the PC Police start recognising that some of their doctrine, from whatever moral high ground they claim to assume, instead of positively achieving peaceful integration, actually hinders its progress, we might then start to break down barriers and achieve a better world. They should remember that points of view other than theirs exist and may even have some credibility—especially if they allow them to bring a smile to their faces!

Despite their well-meaning, but misguided interference, integration and tolerance will eventually happen if it is left alone to evolve. Imposing unacceptable restrictions on our freedom to question (and smile at) what we see as odd in others, is as pompous as it is unwise. It breeds resentment and extremism. We must not be afraid to smile!

The following photograph, said to have been taken in Oldham, is an example of what some may see as amusing and others as offensive.

The compiler of this collection of emails thought long and hard before including it and others. However, his intention is to break down barriers and promote harmony through humour, so if its inclusion offends the photographer or his wives, or anyone else, is this our problem, or is it theirs?

You can't change how people treat you, or what they say about you. All you can change is how you react to it— Mahatma Gandhi.

STICKS AND STONES may hurt my bones but calling names
will not—*Me!*

CONTEMPORARY PHILOSOPHY

**We live in a generation of emotionally weak people.
Everything has to be watered down because it's offensive—
even the truth!**

MANDY

A mother arrived at school to pick up her daughter and saw her
doing hand stands against a wall.

She remonstrated with her daughter, saying, "You must stop
doing that Mandy. The boys can see your knickers."

The following day she noticed that Mandy's hands were dirty.

"Have you been doing handstands again?" she demanded
sternly.

"Yes," replied Mandy. "But I took my knickers off this time."

NEWSFLASH—Birmingham

Several immigrant families died earlier today when a gas
explosion destroyed a block of flats in Birmingham.

The only survivors are thought to be an English couple, Tom
and Mary Smith. They were out at work at the time.

PEANUTS

"Frankie Brown showed me his willy today," said Mandy to her horrified mother. "It reminded me of a peanut."

"Was it very tiny?" asked her mother.

"No. Very salty," replied Mandy.

PARAPROSDOKIANS

These have been included early in this book because readers may be curious to know what they are. Here is the definition:

"A figure of speech in which the latter part of a sentence or phrase is surprising or unexpected; frequently used in a humorous situation or context."

Winston Churchill loved them.

Here are some examples:

Where there's a will I want to be in it.

The last thing I want to do is to hurt you. But it's still on my list.

Light travels faster than sound. This is why some people appear bright until you hear them speak.

We never really grow up. We just learn to act in public.

War does not determine who is right—only who is left.

Knowledge is knowing that a tomato is a fruit. Wisdom is not putting it in a fruit salad.

Evening news is where they begin with "Good Evening" and then proceed to tell you why it isn't.

To steal ideas from one person is plagiarism. To steal from many is research.

Nobody ever goes there. It's too crowded.

Blessed are the censors—for they shall inhibit the earth.

Some marriages are made in heaven—but so are thunder and lightning.

More later.

THE NUMBER 29 BUS

There were plenty of available seats on the Number 29 but a creep spotted a pretty young girl and thought he would sit beside her.

Staring at her breasts, he said, "Is this seat vacant sweetheart?" The girl replied, "Yes—and if you intend to sit there, mine will be too."

Here are some more great put downs:

If you were twice as smart as you are, you'd be half as smart as you think you are.

Your arse must be pretty jealous of all that shit that comes out of your mouth.

Sometimes it is better to keep your mouth shut and give the impression that you are stupid, than open it and remove all doubt.

If I wanted to hear from an arse hole I'd fart.

She got her good looks from her father. He's a plastic surgeon.

...and three classics from the master, Winston Churchill:

A modest little man, with much to be modest about (on Clement Attlee).

Bessie Braddock: "Winston, you are disgustingly drunk."
Churchill: "Yes my dear. You are ugly. But tomorrow I'll be sober."

Lady Astor: "Winston, if you were my husband I'd put poison in your coffee."
Churchill: "Nancy. If you were my wife, I'd drink it."

OVERHEARD....on the doorstep:

"Is Fred in?"

"Sorry luv. We buried him last Tuesday."

"He didn't say anything about a pot of yellow paint before he went, did he?"

NOT SO SIMPLE SIMON

At school the other boys used to get a laugh at Simon's expense because every time they offered him the choice of two coins, a ten pence and twenty pence, he would always choose the ten pence because it was bigger.

"Don't let them tease you like that," advised his teacher when he realised what was going on, "Take the twenty pence next time."

"No way," replied Simon. "Then they'll stop and I'm saving up for a new bike."

SOME GLOBAL FACTS

At any given moment:
79 million people are engaged in sexual activity.
58 million are kissing.
37 million are relaxing after sex.
One lonely bugger is reading e-mails.

MORNING SEX

She was standing in the kitchen preparing our usual soft-boiled eggs for breakfast, wearing only the "T" shirt she had slept in.

As I walked in, half asleep, she turned to me and said softly, "You've got to make love to me this very moment."

Was I dreaming? No, she meant every word. I couldn't believe my luck, so we did it right there on the kitchen table.

She thanked me and returned to the stove with her "T" shirt still round her neck.

Happy, but a little puzzled, I asked, "What was that all about?"

She explained: "The egg timer's broken!"

ACCIDENTAL CELIBACY

After being involved in a serious car accident Barry woke up in a cubicle at A & E to discover that his penis had been amputated. He was devastated.

"This could be the end of my love life" he sobbed to the surgeon.

"I'm so sorry" said the surgeon. "But due to the impact in your groin, it was damaged beyond repair. However, you happen to be quite lucky, because this is the only hospital in the country which does penile transplants. Would you be interested?"

Barry was indeed very interested. "Tell me more." he said.

"Well," said the surgeon, "I have to tell you that the operation is not available on the NHS. It will have to be done privately. But we do have three penises available in the fridge right now which can be transplanted quickly and easily."

"How much?" asked Barry.

"You have a choice" said the surgeon. "There's the standard English model at £2,000, or we have a Scottish one at £3,000 and a West Indian one at £5,000."

Barry, by this time, had cheered up and told the surgeon that he must first consult his wife because they always made decisions jointly in financial matters. He told the surgeon that he would give his decision later after speaking with his wife.

A few hours later the surgeon returned.

"Have you decided what you're having?" he asked, and smiled at Barry's reply:

"Yes, a new kitchen."

OVERHEARD....at WI

"My son flew all the way back from Australia to spend Christmas with us."

"Did you meet him at the airport?"

"No. I've known him all his life."

SEE IF YOU CAN FIND YOUR NAME IN THE WORD-SEARCH PUZZLE BELOW.

Remember that hidden words in word-search puzzles can usually be found horizontally, vertically, diagonally, backwards and forwards.

If you succeed within 5 minutes it is claimed that you are among the top 8% people in the world with high lateral thinking skills.

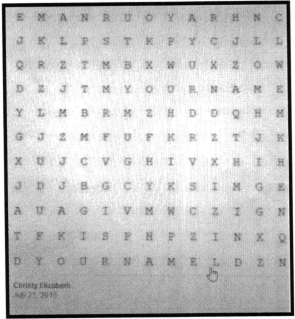

Solution later.

BUDDY

A young woman, disillusioned with all the men she had dated, decided she would stick with Buddy, her dog, for life.

"I wish you were human," she said to him.

Suddenly a fairy flew through the window and granted her wish.... and there before her was the man of her dreams. Tall, dark handsome and sexy.

The young woman was really turned on and couldn't wait to get into bed with her human Buddy. But her urges soon disappeared when Buddy reminded her that she'd had him neutered two years ago.

CHIVALRY IS DEAD

Peter was sunbathing naked on a beach in Jamaica with his hat over his private parts for the sake of modesty.

A woman walks past and says, "If you were a gentleman you would raise your hat!"

"If you were good looking," replied Peter, "It would raise itself."

OVERHEARD—in the playground:

"How come you never do any revision, yet you've never ever failed a maths test?

"When they hold the tests I don't bother going to school."

DANIEL

It was only Daniel's second day at school and his mother was having difficulty in getting him out of bed.

"I don't like it mam," said Daniel. "I don't want to go."

"But you have to," said his mother. "You are the teacher!"

THE MAGNA CARTER

Daniel taught history. He asked one of his brighter pupils where the Magna Carter was signed.

"At the bottom of the page," was one smart reply.

THE MUGGER

On his way home from school one day Daniel was held up at gunpoint.

Holding a gun to Daniel's head, the mugger demanded that Daniel handed over his wallet –"Or you are geography!"

"You mean I'm history, don't you?" said Daniel.

"Don't change the subject!" said the mugger.

OVERHEARD…. in a dark alley:

"I don't like the look of this gang of lads walking towards us."

"No, they look like a bunch of wrong 'uns."

"I'm sure we are going to be mugged."

"Here's that twenty quid I owe you."

SMILE & WALK AWAY

You are going to meet a lot of mean, hurtful and disrespectful
people in your life.
Don't let them hurt you.
Don't let their bitter words break the surface of your skin.
Keep your dignity.
Remain true to yourself and be a better person.
They need help—not you.
It's not up to you to fix them.
Just smile and walk away.

THE LOOK
Stephen kissed me in the Spring
Robin in the fall
But Colin only looked at me
And never kissed at all

Stephen's kiss was lost in jest
Robin's lost in play
But the kiss in Colin's eyes
Haunts me night and day

THE KISS .... definitions

A mutual exchange of salivary bacteria!

....and an AUSTRALIAN KISS?

The same as a French kiss but down under.

....and a GOODBYE KISS?

When leaving the house, 90% of men kiss their wives goodbye. The others kiss their house goodbye when leaving their wives.

OVERHEARD—at the opticians

"My eyesight is deteriorating. I can't see very far these days."

"Okay. Let's give you an eye test. Can you just walk over to the window, look up and tell me what you can see?"

"The sun."

"So, how bloody far do you *want* to see?"

RACIST STORY

Only the most stupid and intolerant people would take offence at the next story which is blatantly anti-English and therefore "racist". Yet if a similar light-hearted story involved someone from one of the more primitive, solemn, or less liberal cultures, some people would be outraged. Why can't these people learn how to laugh at themselves

like we do in Britain, Ireland, Australia, the USA and other more enlightened countries? Why might people in these countries feel relaxed enough to laugh at such "racist" stories against their own countrymen and women, but feel guilty about poking harmless fun at other cultures and their ideologies? Who are these people who decide what and who we may laugh at? On what authority do they seek to censor so called "racist" jokes?

Rivalry between individuals, nations, cultures and the sexes exists and always will do. "Ban the Banter" could be an appropriate slogan for the PC brigade.

If we are *really* comfortable and confident in our cultures, beliefs, convictions and opinions, we should not find it necessary to react angrily when they are questioned, criticised—or even made fun of. Nor should we find it necessary to pass laws to suppress such criticism.

The mature, enlightened reaction to criticism, is to listen to it and, if need be, learn from it—or, if you disagree, then calmly put forward and explain your reasons for being as you are and thinking as you do. The immature, unenlightened, uneducated reaction is anger and vengeance.

It was the Scotland v Wales rugby international in Edinburgh and as the crowds made their way down Princes Street towards Murrayfield, a Rottweiler suddenly lunged towards an eight-year-old girl snarling, with its jaws wide open ready to attack.

The nearby crowd gasped in horror but, quick as a flash, a man in a red shirt jumped out of the crowd, grabbed the dog by the throat and throttled it.

A passing journalist from the *Glasgow Herald* who had witnessed the heroic incident approached the man as the dog lay dead and the crowd cheered in admiration. He introduced himself and said, "That was brilliant. This will be reported in tomorrow's edition. I can just see the headline now:

WELSH RUGBY FAN SAVES YOUNG GIRL FROM CERTAIN DEATH!"

The man replied, "No, you've got it wrong. I'm not here for the rugby."

"Don't worry," said the journalist. "I'll change the headline to:

WELSH MAN SAVES GIRL FROM JAWS OF ROTTWEILER!"

"No, you've got it wrong again," replied the man. "I'm not Welsh. I'm from London."

"Right," said the journalist. "This is my new headline:

ENGLISH BASTARD STRANGLES FAMILY PET."

MY GIRLFRIEND accused me of cheating on her the other day.

I said "You sound just like my wife!"

MISTAKEN IDENTITY—A true (?) report from the *Daily News*.

A Leicester couple's car broke down as they drove into the Asda car park on Tuesday.

The driver told his wife to continue shopping whilst he dealt with the problem.

His wife returned later to find a small crowd had gathered round the car, some of whom were giggling and nudging each other.

On closer inspection she noticed a pair of man's hairy legs protruding from beneath the car and a pair of testicles protruding from his shorts.

Annoyed by the crowd's voyeurism and concerned for her husband's dignity she knelt down and gently tucked the testicles back inside the shorts.

On regaining her feet she looked over the bonnet of the car and found herself staring at her husband, whose testicles were modestly concealed within *his* shorts.

The AA mechanic had to have three stitches in his forehead.

Q. What is a Mexican's favourite sport?

A. Cross Country.

PADDY et al

Paddy thought his new girlfriend could be the new Mrs Right, but after looking through her underwear drawer and finding a nurse's outfit, a French maid's outfit and a police woman's uniform with handcuffs, he decided that if she can't hold down a job she was not the one for him.

PADDY'S PROBLEM

The doctor prescribed some tablets for Paddy's constipation, with instructions to take them in his back passage three times daily.

A week later and with his condition showing no sign of improvement, he went back to the doctor and told him that, as instructed, he had taken the tablets in his back passage. Also in the hall, the kitchen, the living room and the garden shed. "For all the good they did," said Paddy, "I might as well have shoved them up my arse."

PADDY'S SOLUTION?

A few weeks after the doctor had explained to Paddy the correct way of taking his medication, he gave him a follow up appointment to monitor his progress and was reassured by Paddy that his bowel movements were now regular. "Every morning, 8 o'clock on the dot," said Paddy.

"Right Paddy," said the doctor. "I think we've solved your bowel problem."

"Not quite," said Paddy. "I don't get up till 9."

EMANUEL MACRON

The French President was in his helicopter observing the riots in Paris and was touched by the scenes below him and said: "I'm going to throw a hundred Euro note out and make somebody happy."

"Why don't you throw out five twenty Euro notes? Then you'll make five people happy?" suggested his aide.

"Why don't you throw yourself out?" said the pilot. "Then you'll make everybody happy."

BRICKIE'S BUM

OVERHEARD—in the staff room.

"There was a kidnapper in school today. But it's okay. He woke up."

THE PRIVATE DETECTIVE

A man, suspecting that his wife may be having an affair, hired a Chinese private detective to investigate. Here is the sleuth's report:

"Most honourable Sir. You leave house. I watch house. I watch she leave house. I follow. He and she go in hotel. I climb tree. I look in window. He kiss she. He strip she. She strip he. He play with she. She play with he. I play with me. I fall out tree. I not see. No fee. Chung Lee."

THE PARROT

A Chinaman walks into a bar with a parrot on his shoulder and the barman says, "Where did you get that from?"

"China," says the parrot. "There's millions of them there."

A.D.D.

Where do you send a someone with Attention Deficiency Disorder?

A concentration camp.

OVERHEARD....in the synagogue.

"I'm so very proud of this gold watch my grandfather sold to me on his deathbed."

CINDARELLA

The Reverend William Spooner, Dean of New College, Oxford, will be remembered for his propensity to mix up his syllables, often with humorous results and which often took the sting out of his attempts to admonish his students. For example, he chastised a particularly lazy student with "You've tasted a whole worm." There are many more.

So, could this be the reverend gentleman's version of the well-known Fairy Tale?

Once upon a time in an olden day's city there lived a gritty pearl called Cinderella.

City Prindarella lived in a bosh pig house with her father Mr Potter, her wicked and stepful spitemother and her two sisty uglers Chictoria and Varlotte. The sisty uglers were not Cinderella's sisterlogical buyers. They were in fact cyst steppers. You see Mr Potter had lost his worst fife—Motherella's cinder—and remarried.

The new Pisses Me was jealous. She felt threatened by her husband's affection for his cinder Daughterella. She thought her husband biked her letter than her. So when he was out jerking at his wob she cindered Ressarella in drags and made

25

her do all the chasty nores—like dishing the washes, flopping the mores and fleaning out the choir.

Each year there was a royal ball at the kince's prassel and this year Cinderella and the two sisty uglers had invited receivitations. But on the day of the ball Sanderella was sid because her stepful spitemother had given her extra chasty nores to do because she knew that the presence of her beautiful step daughter at the ball would chinder the hances of her own gugly earls in winning the hand of the pransome hince in marriage.

However the recindful Sourcerella worked her bingers to the fone to finish chewing the doors in time. But, alas, it seemed that her hapes were to be doshed. The stepful spitemother had made sure that all Frinderella's socks were cocked up in a lubbard, so she had only her rags to wear. Cheers tickled down her treeks. Was she destined never to preet the mince?

Suddenly there was a light flash of bright and there, fronting in stand of her, was a grand old lady. *"Don't be afraid,"* said the land old grady. *"I am your fairy godmother. I am able to wish you a grant."*

The now cindy Happerella told the old lady that if she were wished a grant it would be to go to the ball. *"Your grant will be wished,"* said the fairy godmother.

"But," explained Sanderella sidly, *"My best cocks are frocked up in a lubbard and I have nothing to wear."*

"Don't worry," said the fairy godmother and with a clap of her hands, Dinderella was pressed in a gowniful beaut and slip glasses.

Then, with a few wagic merds, a pellow yumpkin appeared at the front door and pray hesto, it changed into a colden goach which took Cinderella to the ball.

As soon as the pransome hince eyed claps on her his start hopped and when she hanked her dropperchief he rushed across the room to ask Cinderella to dance.

The night pissed quackly in each other's arms. The cisty uglers didn't cinderise Recognella in her splendid clothes.

But when the strock cluck twelve, Cinderella remembered the winal ferds of the godmother and before the spell wore off and her rock turned to frags, she bled from the fall. In her haste she slipped off her kickers.

The disaprinted poince had forgotten to ask his would be nincess her prame and the next day he set off to identify the gut of the firl that the gas fitter slipped, but when he called at the house the sisty uglers said they were the only ones who lived there.

Prestfallen, the crince was about to horse his mount and ride away when he sinded Spoterella through a side window.

As everyone knows of course, the fit slippered Cinderella's foot, the prince asked her to marry him and this story had a very endy happening.

...and a few more of his "Spoonerisms":
"It is kisstomary to cuss the bride."
"He delivered a blushing crow."
"May I sew you to another sheet?"
"I propose a toast to our queer old dean."

IRISH SEVEN COURSE DINNER?

A six pack and a potato.

BREAKING NEWS

Ireland's worst air disaster occurred earlier this morning when a small two-seater Cessna plane crashed into a cemetery.

Irish search and rescue workers have so far recovered 1,287 bodies and expect that number to climb as digging continues into the night.

THE FLYING LESSON

A young blonde trainee pilot is having her first lesson in a two-seater plane when her instructor has a heart attack and dies.

"Mayday! Mayday!" she yells into the radio. "Help me, help me! My instructor pilot has died and I don't know how to fly."

She hears a voice over the radio saying, "This is Air Traffic Control. We can hear you loud and clear. I will talk you through this and get you back on the ground safely. I've had a lot of experience with this kind of problem. Now just take a deep breath. Everything will be fine. Give me your height and position."

The blonde replies "I'm 5'7" and I'm in the front seat."

After a long pause: "Okay," says the voice over the radio. "Now repeat after me... 'Our father... who art in heaven...'"

OVERHEARD in the red-light district:

"Hello mister. Would you like to have sex with me?"

"Okay, but only if you do it like my wife does."

"I can do it any way you like. So how would you like me to do it?"

"For free."

BETSY'S BIG DAY

Looking stunning in her dress, Betsy smiled radiantly as she approached the church. This was the day she had looked forward to for what had seemed an eternity.

Conscious of the solemnity of the occasion she resisted the temptation to skip happily down the aisle.

Her heart skipped a beat as she approached the altar where Arthur was waiting.

She waited patiently until the priest had finished saying his bit, then leaned over and gently kissed Arthur's forehead.

Then they closed the coffin lid before carting him off to the crematorium.

INNER PEACE

I was feeling a bit depressed so I went to the doctor for some advice.

"One of the main causes of depression," he said, "is unresolved issues. Try to get things off your mind. Always finish things that you start."

When I returned home I looked round the house for unfinished things.

I finished a bottle of Chardonnay, a bottle of Merlot, a bottle of Baileys and a bottle of wum, the mainder of my valinimum scription an a box of choclutz. You has no ideer how fablus I feel rite now.

SCARY THOUGHT

25% of women in the UK are said to be on medication for some form of mental illness.

That means 75% are running around untreated!

THE BALLERINA

Doctor:
"Good morning. So what's your problem?"

Patient:
Well, I'm a ballet dancer and every time I pirouette, I pump. It doesn't smell, but it's still quite embarrassing."

Doctor:
Yes, I can imagine that. Do a couple of twirls for me please."

PIROUETTE/PUMP... PIROUETTE/PUMP

Doctor:
"I think you might need an operation."

Patient:
"That seems a bit drastic, having an operation on my bum."

Doctor:
"No, not on your bum, on your nose—it bloody stinks!"

WIND INSTRUMENT

The First Mate's name was Carter,
He was a musical farter.
He could fart anything
From God Save the King
To Beethoven's moonlight sonata.

OVERHEARD... at the butchers

"A pound of kidley please."

"You mean kidney?"

"I said kidley diddle I?"

THE TAX INSPECTOR

Father O'Malley answers the phone: "Hello, is this Father O'Malley?"

"It is."

"I'm calling from the Tax Inspector's Office. Can you help us?"

"I can."

"Do you know Ted Houlihan?"

"I do."

"Is he a member of your congregation?"

"He is."

"Did he donate 10,000 Euros to the church?"

"He will."

Q. What does a pint of Guinness and a Catholic priest have in common?

A. They're both Irish. They're both black with a white collar... and if you get a bad one your arse will be sore.

OVERHEARD—over a candlelit dinner:

"What would you do if I died? Would you find another woman and remarry?

"Definitely not."

"Why? Don't you like being married?"

"Of course I do."

"Well, why wouldn't you marry again?"

"Okay, okay, I'd get married again."

"That's a very hurtful thing to say."

"Groan."

"Would you live in our house?"

"Sure. It's a great house and you keep it so nice."

"Would you sleep with her in our bed?"

"Where else would we sleep?"

"Would you let her drive my car?"

"Probably. It's almost new."

"Would you replace my pictures with hers?"

"I couldn't expect her to live here surrounded by your pictures, could I?"

"Would you give her my jewellery?"

"No. I'm sure she'd want her own."

"Would you take her golfing with you?"

"Yes I suppose so. They were always good times, weren't they?"

"Would she use my clubs?"

"No, she's left-handed—OH SHIT!"

THE GENIE OF THE SEVENTH HOLE

Playing golf at his local links, Duncan was delighted when his tee shot at the par three seventh hole landed directly in the hole. This was his first ever hole in one. He was to be even more delighted at what happened next.

As he picked his ball from the cup, a genie appeared and said to him, "I am the genie of the seventh hole. Your wish is my command."

Duncan couldn't believe his good fortune. "I would like an enormous penis," he said—and sure enough, as he walked back to the clubhouse he could feel his penis growing and growing, until finally it was protruding from his trouser bottoms by about two inches, which was very uncomfortable, since it trailed on the ground as he walked.

There was only one thing for it. Duncan would have to try and find the genie again. So, for the next several days he spent all his waking hours hitting balls off the seventh tee until, finally, he managed another hole in one.

Again, the genie appeared and Duncan was able to explain his predicament.

"This is not a problem," said the genie. "I will make your penis two inches shorter."

"No, no!" said Duncan. "Can you make my legs two inches longer?"

DUNCAN'S PAL

When Duncan's pal Scott heard about the Genie, he observed that Genies normally grant three wishes and that Duncan had only used two. So he decided to spend hours on the seventh tee trying for a hole in one.

After several weeks his perseverance was rewarded.

Scott had been having some marital problems so he thought that if he was able to provide a luxury house for his wife, all would be well between them.

"I would like a big mansion with a big garden and stables right in the heart of London. In fact, I would like it on the site of Buckingham Palace."

The Genie frowned and explained that this was at the far limit of his magic powers. He asked Scott if he wouldn't mind having an alternative wish.

"Well," said Scott, "what I would really like, is to understand what's going on in my wife's head at times."

The Genie pondered for a while, then said, "How many bedrooms do you want in the mansion?"

THE LATE MICKEY O'LEARY

An American was on a sentimental visit to Killarney in Ireland, the land of his ancestors.

He'd heard of the wonderful golf courses in the area and was keen to have a game there. But he had no-one to play with. So he went along to the local golf club to see if he could find someone to play with.

"I play to a pretty high standard," he explained to the club professional. "So I want to play with someone who will give me a challenge."

"Then that'll be Mickey O'Leary," said the pro. "I'll give you his number."

"That's no problem," said Mickey when he received the call. "I'll be there the morrer at 9 o'clock. But I might be half an hour late."

"That's fine," said the American. "I'll look forward to it."

Mickey duly arrived, on time, with a set of left-handed clubs and beat the American comfortably, winning their 50 Euros side bet.

The American, smarting from his defeat, wanted revenge and suggested to Mickey that they played again at 9 o'clock the following morning. Double or quits.

Keen to earn himself another 50 Euros, Mickey readily agreed, but warned: "I might be half an hour late."

The following morning Mickey arrived, again spot on time, this time with a set of right-handed clubs. Again, he beat the American. This time by a slightly narrower margin.

Sensing the glimmer of an opportunity and determined to get the better of his adversary, the American challenged Mickey to a third game. Double or quits again.

"The morrer it is. 9 o'clock," said Mickey. "But I might be half an hour late."

Curious, the American asked Mickey whether he would be playing with his left-handed clubs or his right-handed clubs.

"Ah, well, you see," said Mickey. "That all depends."

"On what?" enquired the American.

"When I wake up in the morning," explained Mickey, "I look at the wife and if she's lying on her left side, then I play with the left-handed clubs, and if she's lying on her right side, then I play with the right-handed clubs."

"What do you do if she's lying on her back?" said the American.

"Well then," said Mickey, "I'll be half an hour late."

More golf stories later at "LAUGHTER ON THE LINKS"

FUNNY FUNERAL

A very prestigious cardiologist dies and was given a very elaborate funeral by the staff of the hospital where he had spent his entire career.

A huge wreath of beautiful flowers in the shape of a heart lay behind the casket throughout the service.

Following the eulogy, the heart opened and the casket rolled inside. The heart then closed, sealing the doctor in the beautiful heart forever.

At that point one of the mourners burst into raucous laughter. When all eyes turned and glared at him, he said, "I'm so sorry but I was just thinking of my own funeral... I'm a gynaecologist!"

THE TATTOO

A girl called Wendy is curious to find out why her boyfriend had WY tattooed on his penis.

He persuades her to stroke it to find out and she discovers it says WENDY. She is flattered.

They go on holiday to a Montego Bay nudist colony where they notice a black man also with WY tattooed on his penis.

"Is your girl called Wendy too?" she asks him.

"No," he replied. "It says WELCOME TO MONTEGO BAY."

THE TAX INSPECTOR (2)

A tax inspector who was a member of a left-wing anti-Semitic group was sent to audit the books of a synagogue.

"I notice you buy a lot of candles. What do you do with the candle drippings?" he asked the Rabbi.

"Good question," said the Rabbi. "We save them and send them to the candlemakers for recycling and every so often they send us a few candles free."

"What about the biscuit crumbs?" said the tax inspector, determined to find something to catch out the Rabbi.

"Ah, yes," said the Rabbi. "We send them back to the biscuit makers and they sometimes send us free packets of biscuits."

Failing to pin something on the smart Rabbi, the inspector became irritated.

"Well, what do you do with all the foreskins you cut off during circumcision?" he demanded with a sneer.

"Well," replied the Rabbi, "we save them all up and at the end of the year we send them to the tax office—and they send us a complete prick!"

THE PUB LANDLORD

Every Christmas the landlord of my local pub demonstrates the spirit of Christmas for a few days, by actually giving old age pensioners the right change.

PADDY

Paddy bursts into the benefits office.

"I've been ringing 08301730 for two hours. Why doesn't someone answer the bloody telephone?" he demands of the girl.

"Because those are our opening hours, idiot," replies the girl.

GOOD MANNERS

Paul owns a fish and chip shop on Teesside.

One day a yob bursts into his shop, jumps the queue, and demands service with a "Oy fatso, gizza bag of chips!"

"Oh no," said Paul, "you don't get served here with that attitude."

"Waddyer mean?" said the yob.

"I'll show you," said Paul, coming from behind the counter and inviting the yob to swap places, which he did.

Paul then goes outside and re-enters with a polite, "Good evening. I would like a bag of chips please sir."

"Fuck off," said the yob. "You wouldn't serve me."

NEWSFLASH–Liverpool

An assortment of weapons and a stash of drugs, including 20 kilos of cocaine, heroin and ecstasy have been found behind the Liverpool job centre.

The locals are said to be in a state of shock. They had no idea they had a job centre.

OVERHEARD... in the igloo

She was only the Eskimo's daughter but she had an icicle bum.

THE PIG (1)

It was an evening in November
As I very well remember
I was strolling down the street in drunken pride
But my knees were all a flutter
And I landed in the gutter
And a pig came up and lay down by my side.

Yes, I lay there in the gutter
Thinking thoughts I could not utter
When a colleen passing by did softly say
"You can tell the man who boozes
By the company he chooses"
And the pig got up and slowly walked away.

THE PIG (2)

A farmer receives a phone call from his son.

"Dad. I've run over a pig. It's stuck under the tractor still alive. What shall I do?"

"Shoot it," says the farmer. "Then bury it."

20 minutes later the son phones again and says:

"Done that. What shall I do with his speed camera and motor bike?"

PIG FARMING EEC STYLE

This is a letter written to the EEC Rural Payments Agency by Tom Benyon whose excellent charity ZANE does remarkable work in Mugabe's Zimbabwe.

My friend who is in farming at the moment, recently received a cheque for £3,000 from the Rural Payments Agency for not rearing pigs... I would like to join the "not rearing pigs" business.

In your opinion, what is the best kind of farm not to rear pigs on and which is the best kind of pigs not to rear? I want to be sure I approach this endeavour in keeping with all government policies, as dictated by the EU in the Common Agricultural Policy.

I would prefer not to rear bacon pigs, but if that is the type of pig you do not want rearing, I would just as gladly not rear porkers. Are there any advantages in not rearing rare breeds such as Saddlebacks or Gloucester Old Spots, or are there already too many people not rearing these?

As I see it, the hardest part of this programme will be keeping an accurate record of how many pigs I haven't reared. Are there any Government or Local Authority courses on this?

My friend is very satisfied with this business. He has been rearing pigs for forty years or so and the best he ever made on them was £1,422 in 1968. That is, until this year when he received the £3,000 cheque for not rearing any. If I get £3,000 for not rearing 50 pigs will I get £6,000 for not rearing 100? I plan to operate on a small scale at first, holding myself down to about 4,000 pigs not reared which will mean about £240,000 in the first year. As I become more expert on not rearing pigs, I plan to be more ambitious, perhaps increasing, say, to 40,000 pigs not reared in my second year for which I would expect about £2.4 million from your department. Incidentally, I wonder if I would be eligible to claim carbon dioxide credits for all these pigs not producing harmful methane gases?

Another point: these pigs that I plan not to rear will not eat 2,000 tonnes of cereals. I understand that you also pay farmers for not growing crops.

Will I qualify for payments for not growing cereals not to feed the pigs I don't rear?

I am also considering the "not milking cows" business, so please send me any information you have on that too. Please could you also include the current DEFRA advice on set aside fields? Can this be done on an e-commerce basis with virtual fields (of which I appear to have several thousand hectares)?

In view of the above you will realise that I will be totally unemployed and will therefore qualify for unemployment benefits. I shall of course be voting for your party at the next general election.

Mr Benyon has not yet received a response to his letter.

OVERHEARD... in the cocktail bar

"Gin and tonic please barman."

"Sorry sir, we don't open till six."

"OK. Can I just sit here until you open?"

"No problem sir. Would you like a drink while you're waiting?"

Q & A

Q. What does a woman do with her arse hole before making love?

A. Drops him off at the club.

OVERHEARD.... at the psychiatrists.

"Please can you help me?"

"Can you explain what seems to be the problem?"

"I'm addicted to Twitter."

"I'm sorry, I'm not following you."

EQUALITY

Women will never be equal to men until they can walk down the street with a bald head and a beer belly and still think they look sexy.

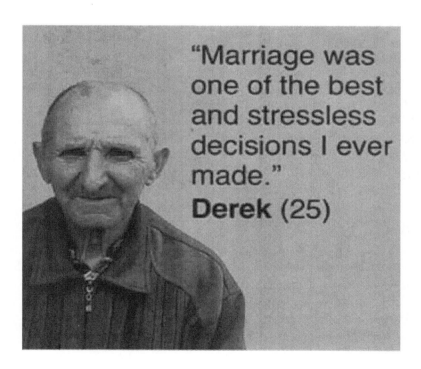

"Marriage was one of the best and stressless decisions I ever made." Derek (25)

MUSIC TO HER EARS—those magic words:

"I love you" and "SALE—50% DISCOUNT"—not necessarily in that order!

Q & A

Q. Why do men go to the club?

A. To forget their problems.

Q. Why do women get together with friends?

A. To talk about theirs!

TEXT FROM MAN TO WIFE:

Sorry I'm late darling. There's a competition in the club to find out who has the most fabulous and understanding wife and I've made it through to the final.

OVERHEARD—at Weight Watchers

"I've stopped using shower gel. I use oven cleaner instead. It says on the bottle "Guaranteed to remove stubborn fat.""

THE BULLY

Little Julian comes home from school crying and tells his dad that he is being teased and accused of being gay by one of the other boys.

"Just punch him on the nose next time," advises dad. "Then he won't call you that again."

"But he's so cute," says Julian.

RIDDLE

Arnold Schwarzenegger has a big one.
Michel J Fox has a small one
Madonna doesn't have one
Mickey Mouse has an unusual one
Obama is one
WHAT IS IT? (Answer on a later page)

THE GOOD SAMARITAN

I saw an old man sitting on a park bench sobbing his heart out, so I went over to comfort him.

"What's the matter?" I asked him kindly.

"I have a wonderful young wife who loves me. We make love every day. She's a wonderful cook and housekeeper and has a well-paid job."

"So, what on earth are you crying for?" I asked and he replied:

"I've forgotten where I live."

MARRIED BLISS?

You have no idea how happy I was when I saw my wife walking down the aisle towards me. "Hurry up," I said. "Get over here quick with that trolley before these cans on special offer get sold out."

You only know what happiness once you're married—and by then it's too late.

If you think women are the weaker sex, try pulling the duvet back over to your side.

A man will pay £2 for a £1 item he needs.
A woman will pay £1 for a £2 item she doesn't need but it's in the sale.

A man has six items in the bathroom—toothbrush, toothpaste, shaving cream, razor, soap and a towel.
The average number of items in a woman's bathroom is 47. A man would not be able to identify more than 20 of these.

A woman has the last word in any argument.
Anything a man says after that is the start of a new argument.

A woman worries about the future until she gets a husband.
A man doesn't worry about the future until he gets a wife.

A successful man is one who can earn more money than his wife can spend.
A successful woman is one who can find such a man.

A woman will dress up to go shopping, water the plants, read a book and answer the door bell.
A man will dress up for weddings and funerals.

A married man should forget his mistakes.
There's no point in two people remembering the same thing.

Fundamentally, a man's life is like his penis—placid, simple, relaxed and hanging free. It's women who make it hard.

...and then God created the female orgasm—so they could moan, even when they are enjoying themselves!

These observations are reproduced courtesy of volume 2 of the bestselling book *How to Understand Women*—Chapter 154, pages 17,378 to 17,380.

THE FAIRY

"We've worked hard all our lives darling. Now that we are in our sixties, I wish we could just sail off and see the world," said a wife to her husband one day. "Yes, that would be great," agreed the husband.

Suddenly a fairy appeared with two tickets for a luxury cruise in her hand.

"I am here to grant your wish," said the fairy, "if that's what you both want."

The wife agreed enthusiastically but the ungrateful husband said to the fairy that he would prefer it if his wife was 30 years younger than him.

With a wave of her wand the husband became 94 years old!

The moral of this story is that men who are ungrateful bastards should remember that fairies are female!

O'REILLY'S TOAST

John O'Reilly hoisted his beer in the air and announced: "Here's to spending the rest o' me life between the legs of me lovely wife."

This was greeted with a roar of approval and was voted the best toast of the night.

"Mary," said John proudly when he arrived home, "at the pub I was given a prize for the best toast of the night."

"Aye, were you now?" said Mary. "And what was your toast then?"

John had to think quickly before he replied:

"Here's to spending the rest o' me life sitting next to me lovely wife in church."

"That was very nice indeed," said Mary, clearly moved by the sentiment.

The following day Mary happened to bump into one of John's boozing buddies who leered at her and said, "John won a prize for the best toast last night."

"Aye, he told me," said Mary. "But I was a bit surprised meself. You know, he's only been there twice in the last four years. The first time he fell asleep and the second time I had to drag him by the ears to make him come!"

OVERHEARD... at Costa

"This coffee tastes like mud."

"Well it was ground this morning."

FOR A MAN TO BE HAPPY

1. It is important to have a woman who is a good cook and a good housekeeper.

2. It is important to have a woman with a good sense of humour.

3. It is important to have a woman who can be trusted and who doesn't lie.

4. It is important to have a woman who is good in bed.

5. It is VERY important that none of these women find out about each other.

...OR UNHAPPY?

Behind every successful man is his woman. Behind the fall of a successful man is another woman.

NEWSFLASH—USA

Experts became concerned about President Obama's mental state when he pledged millions of dollars aid to Northern Ireland following the tragedy of Hurricane Higgins.

THE ART COLLECTOR

A lawyer tells his art collector client:
"I have some good news and I have some bad news."

The client has had a rough day so he asks for the good news first.

"A few weeks ago your wife invested £1,000 in a couple of pictures and she reckons they are now worth £2 million," says the lawyer.

"Wow!" says the client. "That's brilliant. So what's the bad news?"

"The pictures," said the lawyer, "are of you and your secretary."

OVERHEARD… at the Disco

"Look at that bloke on the floor giving it rock all and having the time of his life."

"Actually, he proposed to me twenty years ago but I refused him."

"Looks like he's still bloody celebrating!"

HOWZAT?

When the girl next to me in the bar sneezed, her glass eye flew out towards me and, quick as a flash, I dived down and caught it.

We got chatting and I really fancied her so I arranged to see her again.

After our night out together we went back to her place and made love.

I was a bit disappointed that she seemed so eager so soon, so I asked her if she always made love to men on her first date.

"No." she replied. "Only the ones that catch my eye."

NEWSFLASH

There were angry demonstrations outside parliament today when human rights protesters gathered to protest against not right MP Gladys Thrashem's call to introduce the death penalty for suicide bombers.

The bond between a mother and her young offspring is one of nature's most innate, tender and moving characteristics, as captured in a series of five pictures included in the next few pages.

A MOTHER'S LOVE No. 1
THE OTTER– on the river bank.

CHINESE SICK LEAVE

Wong Chow calls his boss at work and says, "Boss, I no come to work today. I feel sick. I got stomach ache. Legs hurt. I no come to work today."

"I really need you to come in today," says the boss. "When I feel sick like you do, I go to my wife and ask her to give me sex. That usually makes me feel better. Try it."

Two hours later Wong Chow calls again. "I do what you say. I feel great. I be at work soon… you got nice house!"

WHAT'S WONG?

Su Wong marries Lee Wong and soon they have a new baby.

"Congratulations," says the midwife as she places a Caucasian white baby in Su's arms.

"What are you going to call your new baby?" she asks the father, who replies:

"Sum Ting Wong."

2011—A SPECIAL YEAR

July 2011 had 5 Fridays, 5 Saturdays and 5 Sundays.
It had 5 unusual dates:
1/1/11……1/11/11……11/1/11…. and 11/11/11.
This will not happen again for 823 years.

PAT, TOM & SHAUN

There were three brothers from Sligo.

They were very close. They made sure that, whatever happened, they would continue to get together once a week—even after they married and left home.

One day Pat dropped a bombshell. He and his new family planned to emigrate to Australia. There was much sadness in the O'Shaughnessy family.

When Pat arrived in Brisbane and after settling into his new home, his next priority was to find a local pub which served Guinness. Luckily this was within walking distance and Pat's ritual was to go there every Friday night at seven o'clock and order three pints of Guinness, which he insisted were served all at the same time.

After taking alternate drinks out of each glass and the glasses were empty, he would leave.

This puzzled the landlord and eventually he asked Pat to explain this odd behaviour.

Pat told him about his brothers and how they used to have a drink together every Friday before he left Ireland, and how he decided to carry on this ritual in memory of the good times they used to have together.

"What a lovely thing to do," remarked the landlord.

A couple of years later Pat walked into the pub and the landlord said, "Three pints of Guinness, Pat?"

"No, only two tonight," said Pat.

"Oh, I'm so sorry," said the landlord. Is it Tom or Shaun?"

"It's Shaun," said Pat.

"Did he die peacefully?" enquired the landlord.

"Oh, he's not dead," said Pat "He's given up drinking"

RIDDLE ANSWER

What is it? A NAME.

TOMMY COOPER

Tommy Cooper was introduced to the Queen after a Royal Performance.

"Do you think I was funny?" asked Tommy.

"Yes, Tommy," said the Queen.

"You really thought I was funny?" said Tommy.

"Yes, of course I thought you were funny," said the Queen.

"Did your mother think I was funny?" said Tommy.

"Yes, Tommy," said the Queen. "We both thought you were funny."

"Do you mind if I ask you a personal question?" said Tommy.

"No," said the Queen. "But I might not be able to give you a full answer."

"Do you like football?" said Tommy.

"Well. Not really," said the Queen.

"In that case," said Tommy, "can I have your cup final tickets?"

No compilation of this type would be complete without at least a selection of one liners from that legend of comedy Tommy Cooper. Here is the first.

TOMMY—and his car.

Somebody, a complete stranger, complimented me on my driving today. They left a note on my windscreen saying Parking Fine. How nice was that?

A policeman stopped me the other night. He tapped on my car window and said, "Blow into this bag sir." I said, "What for?" He said, "My chips are too hot."

I stopped at some traffic lights and a bloke said, "Can you give me a lift?"
I said, "Sure. You look great. The world is your oyster. Go for it."

On the way home my boss phoned me and told me I'd been promoted.

I swerved.

He rang up a second time and said, "You've been promoted again."

I swerved again.

He rang up a third time and said, "You are now the managing director."

I swerved and crashed into a tree.

When the police arrived and asked me what had happened, I told them I'd careered off the road.

At the police station the officer gave me a thin piece of paper and a pencil.

He said: "I want you to trace someone for me."

I got stopped by the police again a week later.

"I'd like you to follow me to the nearest police station."

"What for?" I said.

He said, "I've forgotten the way."

Next day I decided to take a taxi home.

"King Arthur's Close," I said to the driver.

"Don't worry," he said "We'll lose him at the next set of lights."

When I got home the phone was ringing.

I picked it up and said, "Whose speaking."

And a voice said, "You are."

"I rang up a local building firm and said I wanted a skip outside my house first thing in the morning."

He said: "I'm not stopping you."

So I rang up my local swimming baths and said, "Is that the local swimming baths?"

He said, "It depends where you're calling from."

OVERHEARD... in the house

"When I die darling, I'm going to leave everything to you."
"You already do, you lazy bastard!"

HEALTH & SAFETY

Has H & S gone too far?

Let's be thankful that H & S zealots weren't around in 1805—otherwise we might now be a French colony and have a Napoleon's Column in Trafalgar Square.

Imagine the scenario on board *HMS Victory*—2015 version.

Admiral Nelson:
"Order the signal Hardy."

Captain Hardy:
"Aye aye sir."

Nelson:
"Hold on. That's not what I ordered to Flags. What's the meaning of this?"

Hardy:
"Sorry, sir."

Nelson:
"What do you mean 'sorry sir'? Fetch me that order sheet."

Hardy:
"At once sir."

Nelson (reading aloud):
"England expects every person to do his or her duty, regardless of race, gender, sexual orientation, religious persuasion or disability. What gobbledegook is this?"

Hardy:
"Admiralty policy I'm afraid sir. We're an equal opportunities employer now. We had the devil's own job to get the word England past the censors, lest it be considered racist."

Nelson:
"Gadzooks, Hardy. Hand me my pipe and tobacco."

Hardy:
"Sorry sir. All naval vessels have been designated smoke free working environments."

Nelson:
"In that case, break open the rum ration. Let us splice the mainbrace to steel the men before battle."

Hardy:
"The rum ration has now been abolished Admiral. It's part of the government's policy on binge drinking."

Nelson:
"Good heavens Hardy. I suppose we'll just have to get on with it... full speed ahead."

Hardy:
"I think you'll find there's a four-knot speed limit on this stretch of water sir."

Nelson:
"Damn it man! We are on the eve of the greatest sea battle in naval history. We must advance with all dispatch. Report from the crow's nest please."

Hardy:
"That won't be possible sir."

Nelson:
"What?"

Hardy:
"Health and Safety have closed the crow's nest sir. No harness; and they say that rope ladders don't meet regulations. They won't let anyone up there until a proper scaffolding can be erected."

Nelson:
"Then get me the ship's carpenter without delay."

Hardy:
"Not possible sir. He's busy knocking up a wheelchair access to the foredeck."

Nelson:
"Wheelchair access? I've never heard of anything so absurd."

Hardy:
Health and Safety again sir. We have to provide a barrier free environment for the differently abled."
Nelson:
"Differently abled? I've only one arm and one eye and I refuse to even hear mention of the word. I didn't rise to the rank of admiral by playing the disability card."

Hardy (sheepishly):
'Actually sir. You did. The Royal Navy is under represented in the areas of visual impairment and limb deficiency."

Nelson:
"Whatever next? Give me full sail. The salt spray beckons."

Hardy:
"A couple of problems there too I'm afraid sir. Health and Safety won't let the crew up the rigging without hard hats. And they don't want anyone breathing in too much salt—haven't you seen the adverts?"

Nelson:
"I've never heard such infamy. Break out the cannon and tell the men to stand by and engage the enemy."

Hardy:
"The men are a bit worried about shooting at anyone, Admiral."

Nelson:
"What? This is mutiny."

Hardy:

"It's not that sir. It's just that they are afraid of being charged with murder if they actually kill anyone. There's a couple of legal-aid lawyers on board, watching everything like hawks."

Nelson:

"Then how are we to sink the French and Spanish?"

Hardy:

"Actually sir, we're not."

Nelson:

"What do you mean, we're not?"

Hardy:

"No sir. The French and Spanish are our European partners now. According to the Common Fisheries Policy we shouldn't even be in this stretch of water. We could be hit with a claim for compensation."

Nelson:

"But you must hate a Frenchman as you hate the Devil."

Hardy:

"I wouldn't let the ship's Diversity Co-ordinator hear you saying that, sir. You'll be up on disciplinary report."

Nelson:

"But we must consider every man our enemy who speaks ill of our King."

Hardy:

"Not any more sir. We must be inclusive in this multicultural age. Now, put on your Kevlar vest. It's the rules. It could save your life."

Nelson:

"I'm not sure I want it saving in these circumstances."

Hardy:

"But you must conform sir."

Nelson:

"Don't tell me—health and safety again. Whatever happened to rum, sodomy and the lash?"

Hardy:

"As I explained sir, rum is off the menu. And there's a ban on corporal punishment."

Nelson:

"What about sodomy?"

Hardy:

"I believe that is now legal sir."

Nelson:

"In that case, kiss me Hardy."

OVERHEARD... in the charity shop

"Here's my old hoover for your stock."

"That's very kind of you sir. Don't you use it any more?"

"No. It was just gathering dust."

NEWSFLASH

Thirty wigs were stolen from a beauty parlour in Essex yesterday. Police are combing the area.

A MOTHER'S LOVE No. 2
THE TIGER—in India

RANT

Before we have a rant from a pensioner (nothing funny about this one), let's have a few light hearted quickies to cheer us up.

My wife and I had words—but I didn't get to use mine.

If I agreed with you, we'd both be wrong.

Frustration is trying to find your glasses without your glasses.

A three-year-old boy was examining his testicles in the bath.
"Mam," he asked, *"Are these my brains?"*
"Not yet," she replied.

Ready for the rant now?

Oh Britain, where did we go wrong?

We're broke. We are trillions of pounds in debt. We can't help our own seniors, veterans, orphans and homeless.

If you examine the government's financial assistance policy you will find:

* British old age pensioner who worked hard all her life and paid tax and national insurance for fifty years—**Weekly allowance: £106**
* Immigrants and refugees—**Weekly allowance: £250.**
* British OAP—**Weekly spouse allowance: £25.**

- Illegal immigrants/refugees—**Weekly spouse allowance: £225.**
- British OAP—**Additional weekly hardship allowance: £0**
- Illegal immigrants/refugees—**Hardship allowance: Plus £100.**
- Average yearly totals:
- British OAP—**£6,000.**
- Illegal immigrants/refugees—**£29,900.**

She has a point.

The people in authority who attempt to suppress information of this sort and to make free speech a criminal offence, seem to be incapable of understanding that the ordinary woman who sent this email could possibly have done so from a genuine feeling of injustice. Instead, they often take the attitude that she must have sent it because she hates immigrants and thinks that they should all be deported. This is a dangerous assumption.

Yes, there may be a tiny minority of individuals who do hold such views. But would it not make sense to simply ignore these bigots, unless of course they break the law by inflicting physical harm. Thus isolated, they become impotent.

Instead, by choosing to suppress genuine expressions of frustration, the law makers, by refusing to acknowledge the frustrations and learn from them, actually force otherwise reasonable people to seek a voice through extremist groups and swell their numbers.

Did the incompetent people in authority, whose decisions created the woman's complaint, ever stop to think of the

consequences of their misguided generosity? Were they so lacking in judgement that they failed to realise that situations like this may create resentment?

Is it a failure by them to acknowledge and take responsibility for their lack of judgement and foresight which prompts them to blame those "nasty racist people" like this OAP for having a genuine and understandable sense of injustice?

HAPPY LARRY

Larry wasn't the most cheerful of workmates. Far from it.

But this morning he looked particularly down in the dumps, so they asked him what was the matter.

"Well," said Larry, "the day before yesterday I went downstairs and there was a letter on the doormat saying I'd won £1000 on a lottery. Yesterday I went downstairs and found another letter, this time from a solicitor, saying a long-lost uncle had died and left me a sheep farm in Australia."

"Why are you so unhappy then?" enquired his workmates, to which Larry replied:

"I went down this morning – bugger all."

...& BAD LUCK BOBBY

His dad bought him a rocking horse but it died.

His mam often wished she'd kept the stork and thrown Bobby away.

She used to say that if he fell into a vat of tits he would come out sucking his thumb.

When Bobby's parents got divorced neither of them fought for custody.

He really fancied this girl but she didn't like him. He did make her laugh once though—when he asked her out! She did later communicate with him—by sending him a restraining order.

He had really bad luck with both of his wives. The first one left him and the second one didn't.

He thought he would dabble in real estate but his friend warned him against it. "If you bought a bloody cemetery," said his friend, "people would stop dying!"

Pissed off with his bad luck, Bobby went out one night to get hammered and was knocked unconscious by a bloke with a hammer.

You would have thought that when he died it would have been the end of his bad luck—but he was reincarnated as himself!

THE CONSTIPATED KING

Many years ago in a far off and pleasant land, everyone was happy except the King and one of his subjects, whose name will be revealed at the end of this tale.

The King lived in a luxurious palace and was loved by his loyal subjects. He had a beautiful daughter, the Princess, but alas he suffered from a terrible affliction—constipation—from which he could get no relief, despite all the advice, treatment and potions supplied by the Kingdom's leading physicians.

In desperation a proclamation was issued by the Palace in which the King decreed that whoever could find a cure would be given half of his Kingdom and his beautiful daughter's hand in marriage.

Long queues formed at the Palace gates and hundreds of cures were offered, each one quite ineffective.

The last person in the queue was a shabby nondescript peasant youth who the King was about to dismiss. How, he thought, could a poor young peasant help, where so many wise and educated men had failed? But by then so desperate and despondent, he could not ignore the challenge thrown down by the lad. "Sire," he called out, "I can guarantee a cure for your torment. If I fail, you may chop off my head." Intrigued by the youth's boldness, the King decided to grant him his opportunity. "Follow me," bade the youth with great authority and they set off across the hills into the valley beyond.

Exhausted, the King was about to lose his patience when the youth pointed to an old mine shaft. "There lies your destination, Sire," he announced, "and there you will discover the secret which will put an end to your misery."

The King was instructed by the youth to remove his breeches and place his bottom over the mineshaft, whereupon his bowels instantly disgorged themselves of their hitherto reticent contents.

What rejoicing there was in the Kingdom! The youth's old clothes were replaced with splendid finery and he was transformed into a handsome consort for the Princess.

Each morning thereafter the youth would accompany the King on his journey to his new toilet and one day, curious to discover the secret of the mine shaft's laxative power, the King asked the youth to reveal it.

"Ah," said the prince. "Down there lives a man called Bad Luck Bobby—and everyone shits on him!"

UNLUCKY 4?

I'm surprised this isn't an unlucky number. Nothing ever comes of putting 2 and 2 together.

OVERHEARD... in the bedroom

"Who do you think you're going to pleasure with that little thing?"

"Me!"

WRONG EMAIL ADDRESS

You should always take care when entering addresses in your emails. Errors could have disturbing consequences as a widow in Houston, Texas, discovered.

A couple from Minneapolis decided to go to Florida to thaw out during a particularly icy winter. They planned to stay at the same hotel where they had spent their honeymoon twenty years earlier.

They both had heavy schedules and it was difficult to coordinate their travel arrangements, so the husband flew to Florida on Thursday, with his wife flying down to join him the following day.

The husband checked in and decided to use one of the hotel's computers to email his wife. However, he accidentally left one letter out of the address and without realising his error, sent the email.

Meanwhile, somewhere in Houston, a widow had just returned home from her husband's funeral. He was a minister who had been returned home to glory following a heart attack.

The widow checked her emails expecting messages of condolence from friends. After checking the first message, she screamed and fainted.

The widow's son rushed into the room and found his mother on the floor. As she recovered, she whispered, "The screen, the screen. It's your father!"

This is what he read:

Subject: I've arrived.
Date: October 15, 2009.
To my loving wife.

I know you are surprised to hear from me. They have computers here now and you are allowed to send emails to your loved ones.

I've just arrived and have been checked in.

I've seen that everything has been prepared for your arrival tomorrow.

Looking forward to seeing you then.

Hubby

PS. Sure is bloody hot down here!!!

PADDY THE PUGILIST

Paddy decides to take up boxing so he goes to the doctor for the required medical.

A few days later the doctor telephones him and says, "Paddy, you've got sugar diabetes."

"Great!" said Paddy. "When do I fight him?"

THE POTATO WORK OUT FOR THE OVER 65s.

Forget the gym. Try this relaxing exercise for upper body strength.

Begin by standing on a flat comfortable surface where you have plenty of room on each side.

With a 5lb potato bag in each hand, extend your arms straight out from your sides and hold them there as long as you can. Try to reach a full minute and then relax.

Each day you will find that you can hold this position for just a bit longer.

After a couple of weeks move up to a 10 lb potato bag. Then try the exercise with a 20 lb bag. Gradually increase up to a 50 lb potato bag. Try to get to a level where you can lift a 50 lb potato bag in each hand and hold your arm straight for 1 minute.

When you feel comfortable at this level, put a potato in each bag.

"LOOK AFTER YOUR BODY and your body will look after you"
was the advice my old grandfather gave me. So I gave it everything it wanted—chocolate, alcohol, cigarettes and cakes.
How did the ungrateful heap of flab repay me?
It gave me diabetes and a weak heart!
…and if that wasn't enough, the old fool advised my 65-year-old mother to walk ten miles every day.
We would love to celebrate her 70th birthday this year but we haven't a clue where she is.

PADDY'S GENIE

Paddy was just about to throw out an empty Jamieson's bottle when out popped a genie who told him he could have three wishes.

"I would like," said Paddy, "a glass of lovely Guinness which never gets empty."

Sure enough a glass of Guinness appears with a lovely white head on it and Paddy gleefully downs it there and then and behold, it immediately fills itself up again just as the genie had promised.

"So Paddy," says the genie, "what about your other two wishes?"

"I'll have two more o' them," says Paddy.

MURPHY'S GENIE

Murphy wasn't so lucky when his genie appeared from *his* empty bottle of Jamieson's.

When he asked the genie to provide him with a nice posh house, the genie said, "Piss off Murphy. If I could do wishes like that, do you think I'd be living in a bloody bottle?"

WORDSEARCH SOLUTION

You will find "YOUR NAME" horizontally on line four (the last 8 letters!).

OVERHEARD.... at Marriage Guidance

"Our relationship is based on trust and understanding.

"She doesn't trust me—and I don't understand her."

MOTHER'S LOVE No. 3
THE DOLPHIN—in the Ocean

THE VIRGIN DESK

A crowded Virgin Airways flight from Sydney was cancelled when the 767 was withdrawn from service for safety reasons.

There was only a single desk attendant to deal with the queue of frustrated travellers who needed to rebook their flights.

Suddenly, an angry would-be passenger pushed his way to the desk, slapped his ticket on the desk and demanded to board the aircraft and be upgraded to first class.

The desk attendant politely responded with "I'm afraid that will be impossible sir, but I will try to help you after I've dealt with the passengers who were in front of you in the queue."

The irate passenger wouldn't listen. "Do you know who I am?" he demanded.

The attendant calmly picked up the public address microphone and a message boomed across the airport:

"May I have your attention please. We have a passenger here who doesn't know who he is. If anyone can help him will they please come to desk fourteen."

The applause and noisy laughter from the others in the queue infuriated the pompous arsehole who yelled at the attendant: "FUCK YOU!"

Without flinching she smiled, looked him in the eye and said, "I'm sorry sir, but you'll have to get in a long queue for that too."

THE MALE CYCLE

When I was 13 I hoped one day I would have a girlfriend with big tits.

When I was 16 I got a girlfriend with big tits but there was no passion, so I decided I needed a passionate girl with a zest for life.

At college I dated a passionate girl but she was too emotional. Everything was an emergency. She was a drama queen—cried all the time and threatened suicide if she didn't get her own way. So I decided I needed a girl with stability.

When I was 25 I found a stable girl but she was boring. She was totally predictable and never got passionate about anything. Life became so dull that I decided to find a girl with some excitement.

When I was 28 I found an exciting girl but couldn't keep up with her. She rushed from one thing to another without settling on anything. She did mad impetuous things and she made me miserable as often as she made me happy. She was great fun at first. Very energetic but directionless. So I decided to find a girl with some real ambition.

When I turned 30 I found a real smart ambitious girl with her feet firmly on the ground. So I married her. She was so ambitious she divorced me and took everything I owned.

I am older and wiser now—and looking for a girl with big tits.

Q: Why do they name hurricanes after females?

A: Because when they come they are wet and wild—and when they go they take your house and car with them.

OVERHEARD... at Marriage Guidance (2)

"My wife says I only have two faults. Not listening—and some other shit she keeps rattling on about."

SCOTTISH COW

The Aberdeen Angus cow recently bought in Scotland by a small farming family stopped producing milk so they decided to buy a bull to see if he would mate her to start her milk flowing again.

The exercise wasn't successful, so they consulted the local vet and explained that every time the bull came near the cow she rejected him. If he approached from behind she would turn round sideways. If he approached her from one side she would turn round the other side.

The vet rubbed his chin thoughtfully. Then he said, "Did you by any chance buy this cow in Scotland?"

The family were dumbfounded since nobody had ever mentioned that they had brought the cow from Scotland.

The father said, "How on earth could you know that we bought the cow in Scotland?"

With a distant look in his eye the vet replied, "My wife's from Scotland."

THE INDIAN BRAVE

Three young Indian braves stood before the big chief with mixed feelings of pride and trepidation.

They were to be honoured with their adult status and given their tribal names.

The first one stepped forward and was addressed by the chief.

"You have been given the name of Young Hawk. This is because you have proved yourself vigilant when sighting our enemies and giving us early warning of their approach."

The name Young Eagle was bestowed upon the second brave. "Because you have swooped many times on our enemies and protected us well," announced the chief.

"Step forward Young Thrush," he ordered the third brave.

Then silence.

"Why, great chief, have you given me this name?" enquired the third brave.

"Because you are an irritating c**t," replied the chief.

A MOTHER'S WARNING

"I went into your bedroom earlier and under your bed I found a hood, chains, a whip, handcuffs and a porn magazine. Wait till your father finds out. You'll get a good spanking."

TENDER LOVE?

Sex between two homosexuals with haemorrhoids.

NEWSFLASH

Following a robbery during the night at a local chemist's when the entire stock of Viagra was stolen, a police spokesman said they were hunting a hardened criminal.

MAKING ENDS MEET

Out of work and desperate, a man reluctantly persuades his wife to sell herself on the street.

After discovering she had earned £200 and 50 pence on her first night, her husband asked which ungrateful bastard had only paid 50 pence.

"All of them," she replied.

Q: What do you do with 365 used condoms?

A: Melt them down, make them into a tyre—and call it a Goodyear.

BEETHOVEN SYMPHONIES

As he strolled along Simmeringer Hauptstrasse in Vienna one evening in 1827, a young man heard the faint strains of classical music. It appeared to be coming from Vienna's central cemetery.

Curious, he ventured into the cemetery and searched for the source of the music and was puzzled, and a little scared, to find that it appeared to be coming from one of the graves—one with the headstone inscribed "Ludwig Von Beethoven 1770—1827."

He contacted a friend who was a music scholar and explained this strange phenomenon. The friend rushed to the scene, by which time a crowd was gathering.

After listening carefully, the scholar identified the music as the great composer's ninth symphony, but that it was being played backwards.

The music stopped briefly but was followed by more music. This time it was the seventh symphony, again being played backwards. Then the fifth symphony and finally the second, all being played backwards, all in reverse chronological order of their dates of completion.

They were about to leave and consult an expert on the supernatural in order to seek an explanation, when the graveyard warden appeared on the scene. They told him about the strange event they had witnessed and that they were seeking an explanation.

"Don't bother," said the warden. "I can explain."

The crowd waited expectantly.

"He's just decomposing," said the warden.

THE NATIVE AMERICAN INDIAN, A MUSLIM AND A TEXAN

"I can remember," says the Indian, "when my people occupied the whole of North America."

"My people will soon do that," says the Muslim.

"No you won't," says the Texan. "We haven't started playing Cowboys and Muslims yet."

TELEPHONE MESSAGES

If you are irritated by unwanted callers try this voicemail message:

"Thank you for calling.
I am not available right now.
I am making some changes in my life.
Please leave a message after the tone.
If I do not return your call
You are one of the changes."

OVERHEARD... at the roadside (True story)

A conversation between a traffic cop and a speeding motorist.

"Have you had a drink in the last hour sir?"

"No."

"Have you had a drink at all tonight?"

"Yes, I had one with my meal."

"What did you have?"

"Lasagne."

WOMENS' PROBLEMS

"I've got a problem down below," explained Margaret to her friend Mary.

"Every time I sneeze I orgasm!"

"Are you taking anything for it?" asked Mary.

"Yes," replied Margaret. "Pepper."

NEWSFLASH—local

The manager of the local cinema died yesterday.

The funeral is next Wednesday at 2.10, 5.20 and 8.40.

A CONUNDRUM

Try and work this one out.

A tourist made a provisional reservation at a hotel in a small village. He paid the hotelier £20 holding deposit.

The hotelier gave the £20 to a hooker for services rendered.

She used the £20 to settle her butcher's bill.

The butcher owed the hotelier £20 so he pays it back with the money received from the hooker.

The tourist decides not to take the room and the hotelier gives him back the £20 deposit.

Everybody happy, all debts paid—and nobody's out of pocket.

THIS IS YOUR LIFE—Major Fitzpatrick

This was the title of a 1980's TV programme hosted by Eamon Andrews, which reunited guests of the programme with people who had suffered or enjoyed with them, important episodes in their lives.

A Major Fitzpatrick was one of Eamon's guests. The major had spent many years as a prisoner of war in a Japanese concentration camp and before the emotional reunion was to take place, the Major's story was revealed.

The camp at Yang Jung was run strictly and brutally by the camp commandant Captain Tojo who cut off the Major's leg for trying to escape. This did not stop the brave Major for attempting a second escape. This resulted in his arm also being chopped off.

On both occasions gangrene set in and death would have certainly followed had it not been for Teresa, a sister of Mercy from the Convent at Yang Jung.

Sister Teresa barely left his bedside during his many months of suffering. Her sacrifices were many. All for the life of this brave British soldier.

The Major and his saviour formed a strong bond during his illness and convalescence and it was with great sadness and emotion they were eventually destined to part at the end of the war.

Tears came to the Major's eyes as the story of his awful experiences unfolded and of how this wonderful and dedicated woman, who he had not seen for forty years, had saved his life.

Finally, with a flourish and emotional music, Eamon made the eagerly anticipated announcement.

"Captain Fitzpatrick, here is someone you haven't seen for forty years. Someone who was such an influential part of your life during your incarceration and suffering during the war. Someone who has flown in all the way from Pang Yung to be with you on This is Your Life tonight.

Please welcome **Captain Tojo.**"

...& CAPTAIN SMITHERS

In the greatest days of the British Empire a new commanding officer was sent to a jungle outpost to replace the retiring colonel.

After welcoming his replacement and showing the courtesies—gin and tonics and cucumber sandwiches—as protocol demanded, the retiring colonel said to his replacement, "You must meet Captain Smithers. He's my right-hand man and by God, he is indispensable, the mainstay of this unit. His talent and energy are simply boundless."

Smithers was summoned and introduced to the new CO who was surprised to meet a toothless, hairless, scabby and pockmarked specimen of humanity less than three feet in height.

"Smithers, old man, tell your new CO about yourself."

"Well Sir, I graduated with distinction from Sandhurst, joined the regiment and won the Military Cross after three expeditions behind enemy lines. I've represented Great Britain in equestrian events and won a silver medal in the middleweight division of the Olympics. I have researched the history of..."

"Yes, yes," interrupted the colonel. "The new CO can find all that information in your file. Just tell him about the day you told the witch doctor to fuck off."

ROLF

As the door of his cell slams shut behind him and the lights go out, Rolf Harris puts his head in his hands and reflecting on the wrongs he has committed, begins to sob.

Suddenly, behind him, a voice sings:

"Did you think I would leave you crying, when there's room in my bunk for two?"

OVERHEARD—in the car park

"Dear God, I will give £100 to the church if you find me a parking space.... Oh no, forget it, I've found one."

SUBTLETY?

Some people wouldn't recognise it if it bashed them over the head.

TLC

During his final days, lying in bed, my grandfather talked a lot about how, as a young man, he enjoyed to ski in the Austrian Alps. He suffered terribly from bed sores and my grandmother used to smother his back with oil.

He went quickly down hill after that.

A MOTHER'S LOVE No. 4.
THE ELEPHANT—in Africa

THE CONTORTIONIST

Couldn't make ends meet so he lost his job.

DOUBLE ENTENDRES

Some of the finest aired on British TV and radio:

1. Harry Carpenter at the Oxford-Cambridge boat race in 1977:
"Ah, isn't that nice. The wife of the Cambridge President is kissing the cox of the Oxford crew."

2. Steve Ryder, covering the US Masters Golf:
"Ballesteros felt much better today after getting a 69 yesterday."

3. Mike Hallett the Snooker pundit on Sky Sports:
"Stephen Hendry jumps on Steve Davis's misses every chance he gets."

4. Clair Frisby talking about a jumbo hot dog on Look North:
"There's nothing like a big hot sausage inside you on a cold night like this."

5. US PGA commentator:
"One of the reasons Arnie (Arnold Palmer) is playing so well is that before each tee shot, his wife takes out his balls and kisses them."

6. Pat Glenn, weightlifting commentator:
"And this is Gregoriava from Bulgaria. I saw her snatch this morning and it was amazing."

7. Ted Walsh, horse racing commentator:
"This is a really lovely horse. I once rode her mother."

8. Ken Brown commentating on golfer Nick Faldo and his caddy Fanny Sunneson lining up shots at the Scottish Open:
"Some weeks Nick likes to use Fanny. Other weeks he likes to do it by himself."

9. A female news anchor who, the day after it was supposed to have snowed and didn't, turned to the weatherman and said:
"So Bob, where's that eight inches you promised me last night?"

ED ZACHARY

After four years without even a date, a woman visits the famous Chinese sex therapist Dr Chang.

He says, "Harro. Take off all your croase, get down and craw reery reery fast across floor to other side of room."

After that he says, "OK. Craw reery, reery fast back again."

Dr Chang shakes his head.
"Your problem vewy vewy bad. You got worse case Ed Zachary disease I ever sor. Dat why you get no man."

She says, "Good God. What's Ed Zachary disease?

The doctor replies, "It's when your face look Ed Zachary like your arse."

OVERHEARD… at Easter

"What are your plans for Easter?"

"I'm going to follow in Jesus's footsteps. I'm going to piss off on Friday and come back on Monday."

GOD'S PROMISE

God promised men that good obedient wives would be found in all corners of the Earth.

Then he made the Earth round!

THE BADGE

Did you know that you could download from the internet a kit to make a Border and Immigration Agency badge?

I put on my blue jacket and wore it the other day to visit A & E.

Several people in the waiting room got up and left. So instead of waiting four hours I was seen to in two.

Don't wear it in MacDonald's though. The whole staff disappeared and I didn't get my order.

CATHOLIC DOG

Muldoon lived alone in the Irish countryside with only his pet dog for company. Muldoon was devoted to his canine friend and was devastated when one day it died. He went to the parish priest and asked, "Father, my dog is dead. Could ya be sayin' a mass for the poor creature?"

Father Patrick replied, "I'm afraid not. We cannot have services for animals in the church—but there are some Baptists down the lane who do strange things. There's no tellin' what they believe. Maybe they'll do something for the creature."

"I'll go right away Father," said Muldoon. "Do you think 5,000 Euros will be enough to donate to them for the service?"

"Sweet Mary, Mother of Jesus!" exclaimed Father Patrick. "Why didn't ya tell me the dog was a Catholic?"

SPOTTED—on the Promenade

Man walking along with a cabbage on a dog lead.
He thought it was a Collie!

MARY

Devout Catholic Mary dutifully had fifteen children and when her beloved husband died, she remarried and had fifteen more.

The priest, in his eulogy at her own funeral, praised her devotion and announced, "They will finally be together."

He was interrupted by a member of the congregation asking the priest which husband he was referring to.

"I'm not talking about her husbands," said the priest. "I'm talking about her legs."

PISS POOR

Ever wondered how sayings like this originated?
Prepare to be educated.

In the middle ages they used to use urine to tan animal skins, so families used to all pee in a pot and once it was full it would be sold to the local tannery. If you had to rely on earning an income like this you were referred to as "piss poor", such was the level of poverty in those days. But worse still, if you couldn't afford a pot your family were scornfully derided with "they didn't have a pot to piss in!"

Most people got married in June because they took their yearly bath in May. Brides used to carry a bouquet of flowers down the aisle to disguise the smell. This custom still survives today.

Lucky households possessed a tin bath tub which was filled with hot water when the family could afford it. The man of the house used it first followed by the sons, then the wife, the daughters and finally the babies, by which time the water was so dirty you couldn't see the baby. Hence the saying, "Don't throw the baby out with the bath water."

The staple diet was vegetable stew cooked in a big pot over the fire. More vegetables were added as and when they became available. The pot was constantly boiling and could be days, even weeks old. Hence the rhyme: "Peas porridge hot. Peas porridge cold. Peas porridge in the pot nine days old."

Occasionally, if the family could afford it, a piece of pork would be added but before that it would be hung in the window to "show off" as a sign of wealth or success. So originated the expression: "Bringing home the bacon."

In wealthier households bread was divided according to status. Workers got the burnt bottom layer, the family got the middle and guests got the top—the "upper crust."

Many ordinary people had no way of telling whether someone was dead and often drunks were assumed to be dead and prepared for burial. Many coffins were found to have scratch marks inside. So friends and family would gather round the coffin and wait to see if there would be any sign of life from the "corpse". This became known as the "wake". In fact, some adopted the practise of tying a piece of string to the "corpse's" wrist with a bell on the other end of the string. If there was a sign of life the "corpse" would be "saved by the bell". The person who actually heard the bell would be a "dead ringer".

UNCLE SID

After hearing the latest traffic bulletin, my auntie called my elderly uncle Sid on his car phone asking him to drive carefully because there was some idiot driving along the motorway in the wrong direction.

"There's not just one," said Sid. "There's hundreds of them."

My uncle died peacefully in his sleep ten years later. I want to die like that. Not screaming in terror like the passengers in his car.

A YORKSHIRE LASS

Three friends married girls from different parts of the world.

The first one married a Greek girl. He told her she was to do the dishes and household chores. It took a couple of days for her to get the hang of it, but on the third day he came home to find the dishes put away and the house tidy.

The second one married a Thai girl. Again, at first he saw nothing happening, but soon she had the house spic and span and always had a huge dinner ready for him when he got home.

The third man married a girl from Yorkshire. He ordered her to keep the house clean, wash the dishes, mow the lawn, do the washing and have his dinner ready when he came in.

The first day he didn't see anything. The second day he didn't see anything either. But by the third day some of the swelling had gone down and he could see a little out of his left eye and one arm had healed enough for him to fix himself a sandwich and load the dishwasher. He still has some pain when he urinates.

YORKSHIRE LAD

A Yorkshire rugby league fan was drinking in a bar when he received a call on his mobile to say that his wife had given birth to a 25-pound baby boy.

He bought drinks all round and the celebrations carried on all afternoon, even though some of his pals and the barman were a bit sceptical.

A couple of weeks later he went into the same bar and met the same crowd of lads.

"How much does the little feller weigh now?" one of them asked.

"20 pounds," replied the dad.

"20 pounds?" the barman said. "You told us he was 25 pounds when he was born. What happened?" Tears of laughter followed dad's reply.

"'ad 'im circumcised."

Let's stay in white rose territory for some more Yorkshire tales:

Police have just released details of a new drug craze sweeping Yorkshire night clubs.
Club goers have started injecting ecstasy just above their front teeth.
Police are calling this dangerous practise "E by gum."

A bloke from Barnsley with piles goes into a chemist and asks, "Nah then lad does tha sell arse cream?"
"Aye," replies the chemist, "Magnum or Cornetto?"

At the vets a Yorkshireman asks the vet to treat his cat for worms.
"Is it a tom?" asks the vet.
"Nay, I've browt it with me," he replies.

A Yorkshire woman's old dog dies and because she had become so attached to it and was missing it so much, she asks a jeweller if he can make a gold statue of her pet.

"Do you want it 18 carat?" asks the jeweller?

"No, ya daft bugger," she says. "I want it chewin' a bone."

OVERHEARD... in Boots

"I've heard you sell Viagra."

"Yes sir."

"Can I get it over the counter?"

"Probably. But you might have to take two."

THE ARAB

A conversation between a young boy and his Arab father:

"What is this weird thing we are wearing?"

"It's a chechia. In the desert it protects our head from the sun."

"What about this type of clothing we wear?"

"It's a djbellah. In the desert it protects our body from the sun."

"And what are these ugly shoes on our feet?"

"These are babouches which keep us from burning our feet on the hot sand."

"Tell me papa. Why are we wearing them in Bradford?"

DON'T UNDERESTIMATE THE BOSS.
He didn't get there without being smart.

One successful businessman had an unusual way of choosing a CEO to replace him when he retired.

He called his candidates together and gave each one a seed and said to them, "I want you all to plant this seed, water and care for it and I want you to bring the plant back to me in one year's time. I will then judge the results and from that I will appoint my new CEO."

Jim, one of the junior candidates, became concerned because, despite all his efforts, no shoot appeared. Nor was there any sign of growth after six months. He was convinced he was a failure—particularly since all the other candidates were boasting about how big and healthy their plants were.

Nevertheless, he persevered, changed the type of fertiliser and renewed the soil. Still nothing.

On the day of judgement he was so embarrassed at having to take an empty pot to the boss but his wife convinced him that this would be better than making some excuse. "Better to be honest," she said.

Jim could barely conceal his embarrassment when his colleagues paraded their fine plants before the boss and eagerly awaited his verdict.

"Jim," said the boss. "Congratulations. You are my new CEO. The rest of you hand in your car keys at reception. You're fired."

The others were furious. "How can you promote someone who could not succeed in your task?" they demanded.

"All of you except Jim," explained the boss, "must have substituted a seed for the piece of plastic I gave you. Only Jim had the courage and honesty to bring me the pot with my fake seed in it. Jim is the only one I am prepared to trust as my successor."

- If you plant honesty you will reap trust.
- If you plant goodness you will reap friends.
- If you plant humility you will reap greatness.
- If you plant perseverance you will reap contentment.
- If you plant consideration you will reap perspective
- If you plant dedication you will reap success
- If you plant forgiveness you will reap reconciliation.

SHOW BUSINESS

Little boy comes home from school and says, "Dad, in our school play I've been chosen to play the part of an old married man."

"Never mind son," says dad. "You might get a speaking part next time."

MOTHER LOVE No.5.
THE HUMAN—in the Lidl car park, Easterhouse Glasgow.

OVERHEARD... at the Consultants

"I'm really worried about the operation you are recommending. They say it only has a 25% survival rate."

"Don't worry. You are lucky. My last three patients died."

MEDICAL DEFINITIONS—GUTS & BALLS

GUTS is arriving home late after a night out with the lads, being met by your wife with a broom in her hand and having the guts to ask, "Are you still cleaning, or are you flying somewhere?"

BALLS is coming home late after a night out smelling of perfume and beer, with lipstick on your collar and having the balls to slap your wife on her bottom and saying, "You're next, chubby!"

Medically, both conditions do not respond to treatment and both can be fatal.

OVERHEARD... in Tesco

"I've lost my wife."

"I've lost mine too."

"Shall we try and find them?"

"What does yours look like?"

"Slim, blonde, pink mini skirt and low cut black top."

"Tell you what. Forget mine, we'll both look for yours."

OVERHEARD at an orthodox church elders meeting

"You took a vow of celibacy to atone for your sins but we hear that you have broken that vow."

"When my wife reached up to get something down off a shelf and exposed her knickers I just could not resist and I had to have her there and then."

"Well, we have decided that this excuse is unacceptable. You are now barred from the brotherhood."

"You too? They've barred me from ASDA as well."

BENNY

On his first day at a Scottish school a Muslim boy, keen to integrate with people in his new country, was asked by the teacher for his name.

"Mohammad," said the lad.

"You're in Scotland now son," said his teacher, "we'll call you Benny."

When his mother asked him how his first day went, he told her his new name. His mother was furious. "Are you ashamed of your name?" she fumed and then proceeded to give him a beating.

When he came home from work she told his father and he too gave him a beating.

"What happened to you Benny?" his teacher enquired at school the next day.

"Well, Miss," the boy replied. "Shortly after becoming a Scotsman I was attacked by two Arabs."

SCOTCH CORNER

Let's stay north of the border for some humour which may not be easily understood or appreciated by folk south of the border. Please try though—it's worth it!

A teenage girl phones her dad at midnight and says, "Can you come and get me? I've missed the last bus and it's pourin' wi' rain."
"Okay," says dad. "Where are you ringing from?"
"Fae the tap o' me head right doon tae me knickers," she said.

A Glasgow woman settles down into the dentist's chair.
"Comfy?" asks the dentist.
"Govan," she replies.

What did the Siamese twins from Glasgow call their autobiography?
"Our Wullie!"

After announcing his wedding a man tells his pal he'll be wearing a kilt for the wedding.

"What's the tartan?" asks his pal.

"She'll be wearing a dress," he replies.

A Scotsman in London is having trouble 'phoning his sister from a telephone box.

He contacts the operator who asks him, "Is there money in the box?"

"No. Just me," he replies.

What was the name of the first Scottish cowboy? Hawkeye the noo.

How many Spanish guys does it take to change a light bulb? Just Juan.

A man takes a pair of shoes back to the shop and complains that there is a lace missing.

"No," argues the shop assistant. "Look at the label. It says Taiwan."

What do you call an illegitimate Scottish insect?
A wee fly bastard.

Did you hear about the BBC Scotland series that featured the queue for the toilets at Waverley Station?
It's called the Aw' Needin Line.

While being interviewed for a job as a bus driver, the candidate was asked:

"What would you do if you had a rowdy passenger?"

"Put him off at the next stop," said the candidate.

"Good. And what would you do if you couldn't get the fare?"

"I'd take the first two weeks in August," he replied.

A Glasgow man, steaming and skint, is staggering along Argyle Street when he spots a man tinkering with the engine of his car.
"What's up Jimmy?" he asks.
"Piston broke," replies the man.
"Aye. Same as masel."

A wee Aberdonian loon and his 5-year-old brother are upstairs in their bedroom.
"De ye ken fit?" says the 7-year-old. "I think it's aboot time we started swearing."
The 5-year-old nods his head in approval.
"Fin we ging doonstairs fir breakfast am gang to swear first, then ye kin swear after me—OK?"
"Aye," the 5-year-old agrees with enthusiasm.
The mother walks into the kitchen and asks the 7-year-old what he wants for breakfast.
"Ah'll hae some Weetabix shit!"
SMACK*!!
He flew out of his chair, tumbled across the kitchen floor, got up and ran upstairs crying his eyes out.
She looked at the 5-year-old and with a stern voice, asked, "And what do YOU want for breakfast young man?"
"I dinna ken," he blubbers, "but it winna be fucking Weetabix."

A man walks into a Glasgow library and asks the librarian for a book on suicide.
"Nae chance," she says. "Ye'll no bring it back."

....and a Scottish Love Poem:

A'coorse ah love ye darling
Ye're a bloody top notch bird
An when ah say ye're gorgeous
Ah mean ivry single word

So ye're bum is oan the big side
Ah don't mind a bit 'o flab
It means that when ah'm ready
There's something there to grab

So ye're belly isnae flat nae merr
Ah tell ye, ah don't cerr.
So long as when ah cuddle ye
Ah can git mah arms roond therr

No wummin wha is your age
Hiz nice roon' perky breasts
They jist give in tae gravity
Bit ah know ye did ye're best

Ah'm tellin ye the truth noo
The moment thit we met
Ah thocht ye were as good as
Ah wis iver goanie get

Nae matter whit ye look like
Ah'll aywiz love ye dear
Noo shut up while the fitba's on
An fitch anither beer.

NEWSFLASH. *Glasgow Herald* yesterday

HURRICANE "SENGA"—A DISASTER ZONE DECLARED.

Hurricane Senga hit the Maryhill district of Glasgow in the early hours of yesterday morning, decimating the area and causing £9,000 worth of damage, causing many locals to wake up before their Giros had arrived.

Radio Clyde has reported that hundreds of residents were confused and bewildered, trying to come to terms with the fact that something interesting had happened in Maryhill. Some victims were seen wandering round aimlessly muttering "Pure mental man no?"

One resident, Bernadette O'Reilly, a 15-year-old mother of 5 said, "It gied me an awfy fright so it did. Ma wee Chardonnay Mercedes came runnin intae ma bedroom greetin' but ma youngest two, Tyler Morgan and Natasha Jordan Jade slept through it all. Ah wiz still pure shakin' when I was watching Trisha the next mornin', so ah wiz."

Her neighbour Joseph 'Young Young' McGurn said, "The noise wiz pure deafenin man. At first ah thoat it wiz the young team comin' oota the Bugle Bar, but it wiz even worser."

Several priceless collections of mementos from Benidorm and other popular holiday destinations were damaged beyond repair.

Police say that incidents of lootings muggings and car crime were particularly high that night but calmed down when the hurricane struck.

Forty-two asylum seekers were rescued from an apartment in Elmbank Street. Police intend to search the second bedroom later.

The British Red Cross have so far managed to ship in 4,000 crates of Bon Accord Pola Cola and two tons of cheese toasties to the area to help the stricken locals.

Rescue workers are still searching the rubble and have recovered many personal belongings, including dozens of benefit books and bone china from Poundstretchers who have volunteered to stay open for 24 hours to enable victims to refurbish their homes.

Residents in neighbouring Ruchill offered to accommodate those left homeless but the Maryhill people decided they were better off where they were.

A Council spokesman has indicated that it will probably take a full morning to get things looking normal again and has congratulated residents on their fortitude, adding, "There has been a Blitz spirit. Everybody's been pure blitzed."

The government has pledged to ensure that bookies, pubs, chip shops and other essential services will be restored as soon as possible.

AN APPEAL

An urgent appeal has gone out to try and raise money for food and clothes parcels for those caught up in the disaster.

Clothing most sought after includes:
Fila or Burberry baseball caps, Hoodies, Kappa tracksuit tops (his and hers), Shell suits (female), white sports socks, Rockport boots and Adidas trainers.

Food parcels should, if possible, contain the following items:
Microwave chips, Greggs pies, Sugar Puffs, Tins of Spaghetti, Gypsy Creams, Curly Wurlies, Red Cola, cans of Special Brew and Diamond White, bottles of Buckie or El Dorado, glue or hairspray.

Just 22p buys a biro for filling in the compensation forms.
£2 buys chips, crisps and Irn Bru for a family of nine.
£3 will pay for a pouch of tobacco, papers and a lighter.

BREAKING NEWS

A 10-year-old girl smothered in Alco-Pops has just been dragged out of the rubble. When asked where she was bleeding from she replied, "Craigmont Avenue, whit's it got to dae with you fudd?"

PHILOSOPHY TIME
A good lesson on stress.

A young lady, whilst leading and explaining stress management to an audience, walks round the room with a half glass of water raised above her head.

Everyone knew she was going to ask them the ultimate question—half empty or half full?

She fooled them all.

"How heavy is a glass of water?" she inquired with a smile.

The audience called out answers ranging from 8 ounces to 20 ounces.

"Actually," she continued, "the exact weight doesn't matter. It depends on how long I hold it. If I hold it for one minute, I don't have a problem. But if I hold it for an hour, my arm begins to ache. If I hold it for a day, you'll have to call an ambulance. In each case the weight is the same, but the longer I hold it, the heavier it becomes.

"And that's the way with stress," she continued. "If we carry our burdens all the time, sooner or later, as the burden becomes increasingly heavy, we won't be able to carry on.

"As with the glass of water. You have to put it down for a while and rest before holding it again. When we are refreshed, we can carry on with the burden, holding our stress longer and easier every time we try this practice.

"So, as early in the evening as you can, put all your burdens down. Don't carry them through the evening and into the night. Pick them up again, if you must, tomorrow."

Accept that some days you are the pigeon—and some days you are the statue.

Always keep your words soft and sweet. In case you have to eat them.

Drive carefully. It's not only cars that can be recalled to their maker.

If you can't be kind, at least have the decency to be vague.

If you lend someone £20 and never see them again, it was probably worth it.

Maybe your sole purpose in life is to serve as a warning to others.

Never put both feet in your mouth at the same time—or you might not have a leg to stand on.

Nobody cares if you can't dance well. Just pretend no-one's watching and get up and dance.

Since the early worm gets eaten by the bird, don't be in too much of a hurry.

The second mouse gets the cheese.

When everything seems to be coming your way you may be in the wrong lane.

Some mistakes are too much fun to make only once.

Crayons come in different shapes, sizes and colours. But they all live in the same box.

You are only important to those people who believe you are important to them.

Dwell on the things you should do—not on the things you should have done.

A truly happy person is one who can enjoy the scenery on a detour.

To steal from one person is plagiarism. To steal from many is research.

Do not argue with an idiot. He'll drag you down to his level—and beat you with experience.

Evening News is when the newscaster says "Good evening" and then tells you why it's not.

Light travels faster than sound. That's why some people appear bright until you hear them speak.

Silence is golden. Unless you can improve on it, say nothing.

That's enough serious stuff for the moment. Let's hear about:

THE TALKING DOG

John was sad. His old dog had just died. So he was intrigued to see a sign outside a nearby house: "TALKING DOG FOR SALE."

John rings the bell of the house and the owner invites him to come in and see the dog in the back garden—a lovely Labrador Retriever.

"Do you really talk?" he asks the dog.

"Yes," replies the dog.

After recovering from the shock of hearing the dog talk John asks him, "Tell me your story."

The Labrador looks up and says, "Well, I discovered I could talk when I was pretty young. I wanted to be useful so I told the government I would like to join the SAS.

"In no time at all they had me jetting from country to country, sitting in rooms with spies and world leaders. No one imagined that a dog would be eavesdropping. I was one of their most valuable spies for eight years."

"But all the jetting around and hard work took its toll. I wasn't getting any younger and began to feel tired. They understood. They were really good to me and signed me up for a ground job at Heathrow doing undercover security work. I would wander around near suspicious characters listening in to their private conversations. I uncovered some extraordinary dealings and I was awarded several medals."

"I retired last year, got married and had a few puppies."

John was amazed. He went back into the house and asked the owner how much he wanted for the dog.

"Ten quid," said the owner.

John was flabbergasted. "But this dog is absolutely amazing!" he said. "Why on earth are you selling him so cheaply?"

"Because he's a lying bastard," said the owner. "He's never been out of the garden."

OVERHEARD.... on the Common

"Look at that dog licking his balls. I wish I could do that."

"Give him a biscuit and he might let you!"

OVERHEARD.... outside the Vets

"My dog doesn't eat meat."

"Why not?"

"We don't give him any."

THE MISSING DOG

A couple were devastated when their pet dog disappeared so the wife suggested that her husband should put an advert in the local paper.

After two weeks without response the wife asked the husband what the wording of the advert was. He replied:

"Hey Boy."

Q. Why was the dog happy when it broke its tail?

A. Because every dog has its day, but this one had a weak end!

OVERHEARD... in the pub

"I'm sure I've seen you somewhere. You weren't on a climbing expedition to the Matterhorn in '84 were you, when one of the crampons snapped and we got stranded on a ledge and had to be rescued by a helicopter?"

"No. I've never been to Switzerland."

"Wait a minute. Were you shark fishing in the Indian Ocean in '92? One of the crew was dragged overboard and you dived in and rescued him."

"No. Never been shark fishing."

"Got it! Skiing in the Cairngorms in '77 when we got swept away by the avalanche and spent three days buried before the mountain rescue team found us."

"No, sorry. Never been skiing in my life."

"I've definitely seen you somewhere. Did you serve in Belfast during the troubles when one of the lads got shot in the groin and we had to carry him to safety in a hail of bullets?"

"No. Never been in the army."

"I'll get it in a minute. Were you in here last night?"

"Yes"

"Ah. That's where I've seen you!"

PADDY'S BIRTHDAY

Paddy was aware of vague tales of his ancestors' amazing claim to fame. Many, who were the eldest sons had, apparently, on their 18th birthday, been able to walk on water.

So on his 18th birthday Paddy and his pal Mick had taken a boat out into the middle of a nearby lough. He stepped out of the boat and nearly drowned.

Mick just barely managed to pull him to safety.

Furious and confused, Paddy went to see his grandmother.

"Grandma," he asked, "'tis me 18th birthday, so why can't I walk 'cross the lough like me father, his father and his father before him?"

Granny looked deeply into Paddy's troubled eyes and said:

"Your father, your grandfather and your great grandfather were all born in January when the lough was frozen over, not in August like you, you loon."

PADDY & MICK

"Look here," said Paddy to his pal Mick while they were out for a walk one day. "This feller must have been killed in a car accident. They've buried him by the roadside."

"What's it say on his headstone?" said Mick.

"Jaysus," said Paddy. "The feller was 152 when he died."

"What was his name?" asked Mick.

"Miles, from London," replied Paddy.

Time for another RANT

You are a senior citizen and your Local Authority says they are going to sell your house to pay for your nursing care. So what do you do?

Our plan is to give everyone over 65 a gun and four bullets. You use them to shoot four politicians.

Of course, this means you will be sent to prison where you will get three meals a day, a roof over your head, central heating, air conditioning and all the health care you need.

Need new teeth? No problem. Need glasses? OK. Need new hip, knees, kidney, lungs or heart? They're all covered.

As an added bonus your kids can come and visit you as often as they do now.

And who pays for all this? The same government that just told you that they cannot afford to pay for your nursing care!

Plus, because you are a prisoner, you don't have to pay income tax and you get to keep your house.

And you get rid of four useless politicians!

So, in reality, health care is only free for citizens who don't own a house or have savings and who, instead, choose to

spend all their money on booze, cigarettes and holidays in Benidorm. Or for those who have protected their assets through tax havens or loopholes in the rules.

No wonder the sender of this email is bitter.

Q: Why do politicians make promises like "free health care for all" when the country cannot afford it?

A: Because we fall for lies like this and vote for them.

JANICE & SUE'S TELEPHONE CHAT

"Hi Jan. How's things?"

"Just wonderful, Sue."

"Sounds interesting. Tell me."

"Well, when I got in from work yesterday John had done the washing and ironing and hoovered through."

"Wow. How did you persuade him to do that?"

"Didn't have to. Apparently, he'd read somewhere that the reason working women don't often make love is because they are too tired combining work with household chores."

"That's right."

"Yes, but there's more. He made us all a lovely dinner, did the washing up, helped the kids with their homework, bathed them and put them to bed."

"Go on. Tell me what happened in bed."

"Nothing. He was too tired!"

72 VIRGINS?

Muslim suicide bombers in Britain are set to begin a three-day strike next Monday in a dispute over the number of virgins they are entitled to in the afterlife.

Emergency talks with Al Qaeda have so far failed to produce an agreement.

The unrest began last Tuesday when Al Qaeda announced that the number of virgins a suicide bomber would receive after his death will reduce from 72 to 40. The rationale for the cut was the increase in recent years of the number of suicide bombings and a subsequent shortage of virgins in the afterlife.

The suicide bombers' union, the British Organisation of Occupational Martyrs (B.O.O.M), responded with a statement that this was unacceptable to its members and immediately called for strike action.

General Secretary Abdullah Amir told the press: "Our members are literally working themselves to death in the name of Jihad. We don't ask much in return, but to be treated like this is a kick in the teeth."

Speaking from his shed in Tipton in the West Midlands, England, where he currently resides, an Al Qaeda chief executive explained: "We sympathise with our workers' concerns but Al Qaeda is simply not in a position to meet these demands. They are simply not accepting the realities of modern-day Jihad in a competitive market place.

"Thanks to Western depravity, there is now a chronic shortage of virgins in the afterlife. It's a straight choice between reducing expenditure and laying people off. I don't like cutting wages but I'd hate to have to tell 3000 of my staff that they won't be able to blow themselves up."

Spokesmen for the union in Newcastle, Middlesbrough, Essex, Glasgow and Plymouth stated that they would be unaffected by the cuts as there were no virgins in their areas anyway.

Apparently, the drop in the number of suicide bombers has been largely put down to the emergence of a certain Scottish singing star. Now that Muslims know what a virgin looks like they are no longer so keen to go to paradise.

EXTRACTS FROM...

1. School Reports.

Since my last report, your son has reached rock bottom and has started to dig.

Your child has delusions of adequacy.

Your son sets low personal standards and then consistently fails to achieve them.

Your child brings smiles to the faces of his classmates—every time he leaves the room.

2. Police Videos.

You know, stop lights don't come any redder than the one you just went through.

If you run you'll only go to jail tired.

Can you run faster than 1200 feet per second? Because that's the speed of the bullet that'll be chasing you.

Fair? You want me to be fair? Listen, Fair is a place where you go to ride on rides, eat candy floss and step in monkey poo.

I'm glad to hear that the Chief Constable is a personal friend of yours. So you have someone who can stand bail for you. Lucky you.

You didn't think we gave tickets to pretty women eh? You're right. Sign here.

3. Letters to Local Councils.

It's the dogs' mess I find hard to swallow.

Their 18-year-old son is continually banging his balls against my fence.

My lavatory seat is cracked. Where do I stand?

50% of the walls are damp, 50% have crumbling plaster and 50% are just plain filthy.

The toilet is blocked and we can't bath the children until it is cleared.

Our kitchen floor is damp. We have two children and we would like a third, so please send somebody round to do something about it.

I am a single woman living in a downstairs flat and would you please do something about the noise made by the man on top of me every night.

This is to let you know our toilet seat is broken and we can't get BBC2.

4. GCSE Exam papers.

Q. Name four seasons.
A. Salt, pepper, mustard and vinegar.

Q. What guarantees might a mortgage company insist on?
A. If you are buying a house they will insist you are well endowed.

Q. Name a major disease associated with cigarette smoking.
A. Premature death.

Q. What is artificial insemination?
A. When the farmer does it to the bull instead of the cow.

Q. What is a terminal illness?
A. When you are sick at the airport.

Q. What is a fibula?
A. A small lie.

Q. What is a turbine?
A. Something an Arab wears on his head.

5. Notes in milk bottles (for those who can remember them).

Please close the gate behind you because the birds keep pecking off the tops.

Sorry about yesterday's note. I didn't mean one egg and a dozen pints. I meant the other way round.

Please send me a form for free milk. I have a two-year-old baby and didn't know about it until a neighbour told me.

From now on please leave two pints every other day and one pint on the days in between, except Wednesdays and Saturdays when I don't want any milk.

No milk. Please do not leave milk at No 14 either as he is dead until further notice.

Sorry not to have paid your bill before but my wife had a baby and I have been carrying it around in my pocket.

6. From a mother to her son's teacher:

Harry is sorry he didn't do his homework last night. He will never do it again.

THE LOCUM

A doctor in Dublin wanted a day off to go fishing, so he seconded a locum from another surgery.

"Murphy," he says to the Locum, "be sure to look after me patients, won't you? I want a report for every patient."

127

"Be sure I will," replies Murphy.

On the doctor's return, Murphy starts to go through the list.

"The first one was suffering from headaches so he was. I gave him Paracetamol.

"The second one had indigestion so I gave him Gaviscon.

"Then, as I was sitting there writing up me notes, a gorgeous young woman borsts in so she does. Like a bolt outa the blue she tears off her clothes and lies down on the table, spreads her legs and shouts, 'For the love of Saint Patrick I have not seen any man for ages.'"

"Tunderin' Lard, Murphy me boy, what did ye do?"

"I put some drops in her eyes."

THE STRANGER

A few years after I was born my dad met a stranger who was new to our small town. From the beginning dad was so fascinated with this enchanting newcomer that he invited him to live with our family. The stranger was readily accepted and was around from then on.

As I grew up I never questioned his place in my family. In my young mind he had a special niche. Mother taught me good from evil. My father taught me obedience. But the stranger... he was our story teller. He would keep us spellbound for hours on end with adventures, mysteries and comedy.

If I wanted to know anything about politics, history or science, he always knew the answers to the past and even seemed to be able to predict the future! He took my family to our first major league ball game. He made me laugh and he made me cry. But dad didn't seem to mind.

Sometimes mom would get up quietly while the rest of us were shushing each other to listen to what he had to say, and she would go to the kitchen for some peace and quiet.

I wonder now whether she ever prayed for the stranger to leave.

Dad ruled the household with certain moral convictions but the stranger never felt obligated to honour them. Profanity for example, was never allowed in our home—not from us, our friends or visitors. Our long-term visitor however, got away with four letter words that burned my ears and made my dad squirm and my mother blush.

My dad didn't permit the liberal use of alcohol but the stranger tried to encourage us to try it on a regular basis. He made cigarettes look cool, cigars manly and pipes distinguished.

He talked freely (much too freely) about sex. His comments were sometimes blatant, sometimes suggestive and generally embarrassing.

I now know that my concepts about relationships were influenced strongly by the stranger. Time after time he opposed the values of my parents, yet he was seldom rebuked—and NEVER asked to leave.

More than fifty years have passed since the stranger moved in with our family. He has blended right in and he is not nearly as fascinating as he was at first. Still, if you could walk into my parents' den today, you would still find him sitting over in his favourite corner, waiting for someone to listen to him talk and watch him draw his pictures.

His name?
We just call him TV

He has a wife now.
We call her computer

They have three children—cell phone, ipod and ipad.

OVERHEARD... at the police station

"I want to report a theft of my wife's credit card, officer."

"When did the theft occur, sir?"

"Three years ago."

"Three years? Why has it taken so long for you to report the theft?"

"The thief spends less than my wife did."

F1 NEWS

Formula 1 giants Ferrari have today sacked their entire pit crew following recent poor results.

The announcement followed Ferrari's decision to take advantage of the British government's "Work for your Dole" scheme and employ youths from the Merseyside area.

The decision to hire them was brought about by a recent ITV documentary on how unemployed youths from Toxteth were able to remove a set of wheels in less than 6 seconds, even without proper equipment, whereas Ferrari's existing crew, after many hours of practise using sophisticated gear, could only do it 8 seconds.

The plan was to give Ferrari the edge in this keenly competitive sport where many races were won and lost in the pit lane.

However, Ferrari got more than they bargained for. At the crew's first practise session, not only was the Scouse pit crew able to change all four wheels in under 5 seconds, but within 12 seconds they had resprayed, rebadged and sold their car to the McLaren team for 8 cases of Stella, a bag of weed and a photo of Lewis Hamilton's bird in the shower.

POINTLESS QUESTION

One hundred people from Liverpool were asked today if Britain should change its currency. 98% said no, they were happy with the Giro.

DO NOT BEND

One of the Scousers received a letter in the post. It said DO NOT BEND. He's still figuring out how to pick it up.

MASTERCARD WEDDING

A true story of a very unusual wedding reception which took place at Clemson University in the USA.

After the reception meal the bridegroom got up onto the stage with the microphone to address the guests. He said he wanted to thank them for coming, many from long distances, to support him and his bride. He especially wanted to thank his new father-in-law for providing such a lavish reception which, he understood, cost $32,000. He also said how much he appreciated him for paying for the deluxe honeymoon which, he understood, cost $8,500. To say nothing of the wedding photographs and the bride's dress.

As a token of his deep appreciation he said he wanted to give everyone a special gift, just from him and he asked all the guests to open the envelopes taped under their chairs.

Inside each manila envelope was an 8 x 10 glossy photograph of his bride having sex with the best man, taken by a private detective he had hired when he became suspicious. After enjoying the looks of astonishment and disgust on everyone's face, he turned to his best man and said, "Farewell to you." He then looked at his dumbfounded bride and said, "Farewell to you too."

He then walked out and immediately had the marriage annulled. He had carried out this charade to exact revenge on his wife's family and to tarnish the reputation of her and his best man.

There are some things money can't buy. For everything else there's Mastercard!

Life isn't like a bowl of cherries.
It's more like a jar of Jalapenos.
What you do today,
Might burn your arse tomorrow.

LAST RIGHTS?

When Morris discovered that he had only 24 hours to live, he and his wife Louise went out and dined at the finest restaurant in town.

When they went to bed that night Louise was only too happy for Morris to have sex but when he demanded it for the third time, she became a little irritated and turned over and went to sleep.

However, an hour later Morris woke her up demanding more sex, reminding her that he then had only four hours to live, so she reluctantly obliged before settling down to sleep.

Morris couldn't sleep. Worried about his impending death he tossed and turned and couldn't resist waking his wife again, saying, "Honey. I only have two hours to live. Do you think we could...?"

At this point his wife's patience ran out and she snapped: "Listen Morris, enough is enough. I have to get up in the morning. You don't."

LONELY HEARTS

Ad in the dating column of a newspaper:

"Caring, considerate, sympathetic, tolerant, open minded, sensitive and undemanding gentleman seeks female for companionship."
Box 123, Port Banyon Gazette.
PS. No fatties.

WEALTH

Wealth is the slave of the wise man. The master of a fool.
Seneca

I think you will find, when death takes its toll,
All the money you made won't buy back your soul.
Bob Dylan

If wealth was the result of sacrifice, hard work and enterprise, every woman in Africa would be a millionaire.
George Monbolt

Too many people spend money they earn to buy things they don't want, to impress people they don't like.
Will Rogers

Wealth consists not of having great possessions, but having few wants.
Epictetus

Money can't buy you friends, but you can get a better class of enemy.
Spike Milligan

Money doesn't make people happy. People make people happy.
Steve Wynn

WHERE'S KITTY?

You have five minutes to find the cat hidden in this picture:

Clue: She is white with a black back and head.

NEWSFLASH—Iquitos, Peru

There were no survivors from the Peruana Airlines plane which crashed yesterday killing all 152 people on board. Both families are devastated.

INSURANCE POLICY

A Jewish businessman decided not to insure his factory against flood—because he didn't know how to start one.

He wouldn't insure the office clock against theft either—because his workers never took their eyes off it.

He and his partner walked into a bar. It was busy. So they bought it.

What do you call a Jewish stock take? A fire.

JOHN 5. 29

And God said unto John, come forth and receive eternal life.

Unfortunately, he came fifth and won a toaster.

TOMMY—at the doctors

A man walks into the doctors.
The doctor said, "I haven't seen you in a long time."
The man replied, "I know. I've been ill."

Man goes to the doc with a strawberry growing out of his head. Doc says: "I'll give you some cream to put on it."

Guy goes into the doctors and says, "I've got a cricket ball stuck up my backside."
"How's that?"
"Don't you start."

I went to the doctors the other day.
I said, "With all the excitement of Christmas I can't sleep."
He said, "Try lying on the edge of the bed. You'll soon drop off."

I went to the doctors the other day and he told me I had a serious illness.
"I want a second opinion," I said.
He said, "Alright. You're ugly as well."

WHAT CONFUCIUS DID NOT SAY

Passionate kiss, like spider's web, leads to undoing of fly.

Woman who goes camping must beware of evil intent.

Man who runs in front of car gets tired. Man who runs behind car gets exhausted.

Man who eats many prunes gets good run for money.

Man who drives like hell is bound to get there.

It takes many nails to build a crib but only one screw to fill it.

Man who stands on toilet is high on pot.

Man with only one chopstick go hungry.

APPLE DO IT AGAIN

Apple Computer announced today that they have developed a computer chip that can store and play high fidelity music in women's breast implants.

The iTIT will cost between £499 and £699 depending on speaker size.

This was welcomed by women all over the world as a major breakthrough in their relationship with men, since they have always complained about them staring at their tits and not listening to them.

DRESS CODE

An Englishman, a Scotsman, a Welshman, an Irishman, a Latvian, a Turk, an Aussie, a Spaniard, a Greek, an Italian, a Yank, a Mexican, a Jap, a Pole, a Serb, a Lithuanian, a Chinaman, a German, an Argentinian, a Frenchman, a Korean and a Swiss man tried to get into a nightclub but the bouncer wouldn't let them in without a Thai.

OVERHEARD—at the bank

"I would like to borrow some money."

"I'm afraid the loan arranger isn't in today sir.

"OK. Can I speak to Tonto then?"

THE HOTEL BILL

A woman decided to treat herself to an overnight stay in one of Chicago's best hotels.

When she checked out she was presented with a bill for $250.

She was furious. It was a nice hotel but the room was certainly not worth $250—and without breakfast too.

The desk clerk pointed out that this was the standard rate but the woman wasn't happy and demanded to see the manager who, in justification of the price, explained the hotel facilities—the Olympic size pool, a fitness room, conference centre, etc., etc.

"But I didn't use them," the woman complained.

"Well you could have used them," said the manager. "The hotel is also famous for its shows. We have the best entertainment from New York, Las Vegas and all over the world."

"But I didn't go to any of the shows," insisted the woman.

No matter how many hotel amenities the manager described, she told him that she had not used any of them. Each time the manager responded with, "Well, they were available, so you could have used them."

The manager, unmoved by the woman's insistence, demanded payment, so the woman wrote out a cheque and handed it to him.

"But this cheque is made out for only $50," said the manager.

"That's correct," said the woman. "I have charged you $200 for having sex with me."

"But I didn't have sex with you!" he said.

"Well," said the woman, "the facility was available but you chose not to use it."

Let's stay in the USA for the next few—the first a report from the local Augusta newspaper under the headline "Assailant suffers injuries from fall."

WHODUNNIT?

Orville Smith, a store manager for Best Buy in Augusta. Ga., told police he observed a male customer, later identified as Tyrone Jackson of Augusta, on surveillance cameras putting a laptop computer under his jacket. When confronted the man became irate, knocked down an employee, drew a knife and ran for the door.

Outside on the sidewalk were four marines collecting toys for the Toys for Tots program. Smith said the marines stopped the man, but he stabbed one of the marines, Cpl Phillip Duggan, in the back. The injury did not seem to be severe.

After the police and an ambulance arrived at the scene, Cpl. Duggan was transported for treatment.

The subject was also transported to the local hospital with two broken arms, a broken ankle, a broken leg, several missing teeth, possible broken ribs, multiple contusions, assorted lacerations, a broken nose and a broken jaw... injuries he sustained when he slipped and fell off the curb after stabbing the marine, according to a police report.

OVERHEARD... at the speech therapists

"I can't pronounce my F's, T's and H's."

"Well you can't say fairer than that."

ACCIDENTAL REVENGE—a wife's letter

To my darling husband.

Before you return from your overseas trip I just want to tell you about the small accident I had with your new pickup truck when I turned into the driveway. Probably not too bad and I really didn't get hurt so I don't want you to worry too much about me.

I was coming home from Sylvan Park and when I turned into the drive I accidentally pushed down on the accelerator instead of the brake.

The garage door is slightly bent but the pickup fortunately came to a halt when it crashed into the classic car that you have been carefully restoring.

I really am sorry, but I know how much you love me and as a lovely faithful husband I know you will forgive me.

From your darling wife Carla.

PS. By the way your girlfriend telephoned.

HARVEY'S HARLEY

Harvey saved for years to buy a Harley Davison. He couldn't afford a new one and the used ones he could afford were always in poor condition. Until one day, not able to believe his luck, he came across a pristine 10-year-old model at a good price so he bought it.

He asked the seller how he had kept it in such good condition for all those years and the seller explained that whenever he was out on the bike and it started to rain he rubbed Vaseline on the chrome.

He couldn't wait to show his girlfriend Sandra his new possession and when he telephoned her with the news, she invited him, for the first time, to dinner with her parents.

When dinner was nearly over Sandra explained their family little "game" where the first one to speak had to do the washing up.

When the meal was over they settle down in front of the television and Harvey cuddles up to Sandra, kisses her and when he finds no response or objections, fondles her breasts. Still nobody objects, so he becomes bolder, reaches up her skirt and removes her knickers. Not a word. So he takes her right there on the sofa in front of her parents. Still not a word.

Harvey couldn't believe it and starts eyeing Sandra's attractive mother. He then sits next to her and repeats his advances, still with no objection forthcoming. So he has his way with her too.

Hearing rain drops outside, he gets up and takes a jar of Vaseline from his pocket.

"I'LL DO THE BLOODY DISHES!" screeches the father.

ITALISPEAK

A lady was seated behind two Italians in a bus and couldn't help overhearing their conversation, which went something like this:

Emma come first.
Den I come
Two asses come together.
Once amore
Two asses come together
Again and pee twice
I come a one alasta time.

The lady became annoyed and told them sternly that in America they should not embarrass people by talking about your sex lives in public.

"Hey. Calma down lady," said one of the Italians. "Whooza talking about a sex? I ama justa tellin' mya frienda how to spella Mississipi."

OVERHEARD... in the park

"Does your dog bite?"

"No"

"I'll stroke him then. OUCH!!!!!   I thought you said your dog didn't bite."

"It's not my dog."

A GRANDDAUGHTER'S PRAYER

Dear God. Please send some clothes to the girls on granddad's computer.

...& HER WEEKLY OUTING

Old Tommy loved his 5-year-old granddaughter.
Every Saturday he would take her out to interesting places, have a nice lunch or picnic and buy her ice cream, candy floss and sweets. She loved it
But one day her grandfather had a terrible cold and had to stay in bed so her grandmother took her instead.
When they returned she rushed up to see her grandfather. He asked her how her day had gone.

"It was OK," she replied, "but it was a bit boring. We didn't see any arseholes, or queers, or pieces of shit, or blind bastards or Muslim camel humpers. We just drove around and grandma smiled at everybody."

BIBLICAL PROPHESY

In two separate enactments Washington County in the USA legalised gay marriage and marijuana, thus fulfilling the prophesy in Leveticus 20:13—"If a man lay with another man they should be stoned."

BATH NIGHT

A Scottish couple took in an 18-year-old girl as a lodger. She asked if she could have a bath, but the woman of the house said they didn't have a bath but, if she wanted to, she could use the tin tub in front of the fire.

"Monday night's the best night when my husband goes out to darts," she said.

The following Monday the girl got undressed for her bath and the wife commented on the fact that she had no pubic hair. "It's always been like that," explained the girl.

She told her husband about it later when he came in but he didn't believe her so the wife suggested that the following Monday he should hang around outside before going to darts and she would leave a gap in the curtains so he could have a peek.

The girl was curious and asked the wife why she had commented on her lack of hair. She thought that was normal.

"No, no," said the wife and she lifted her nightdress and showed the girl her bush.

Later that night when the husband came in, she asked him, "Did you see it?"

"Yes," he said, "but why on earth did you have to show her yours?"

"Why ever are you worried about that?" she said. "You've seen it often enough before."

"I know," he said. "But the darts team hadn't."

PARENTAL ADVICE

APPRECIATE A JOB WELL DONE:
"If you're going to kill each other, do it outside… I've just finished cleaning."

RELIGION:
"You'd better pray that will come out of the carpet."

LOGIC:
"Because I said so, that's why."

TIME TRAVEL:
"If you don't straighten up, I'll knock you into the middle of next week."

MORE LOGIC:
"If you fall out of that swing and break your neck I won't be taking you to the shop."

IRONY:
"Keep crying and I'll give you something to cry about."

CONTORTIONISM:
"Will you look at that dirt on the back of your neck."

STAMINA:
"You'll sit there till all those sprouts are gone."

WEATHER:
"This room looks like a tornado had hit it."

HYPOCRISY:
"I've told you a million times—don't exaggerate."

ENVY:
There are millions of children out there who don't have wonderful parents like you do."

ANTICIPAION:
"Just wait till I get you home."

RECEIVING:
"You're going to get it when your father gets in!"

HUMOUR:
"When the lawnmower cuts off your toes don't come running to me."

BECOMING AN ADULT:
"If you don't eat your vegetables you'll never grow up."

GENETICS:
"You're just like your father."

MY ROOTS:
"Close that door. Do you think you were born in a barn?"

WISDOM:
"When you're as old as me you'll understand."

THAT TIME OF LIFE

A woman in her fifties became deeply concerned with symptoms she simply could not understand and wasn't able to share with her family or friends because, she thought, they simply would not take her seriously.

She eventually plucked up courage and made an appointment with a Gynaecologist.

She was certain he would not understand or believe her either, but he assured her that for many years he had dealt with many unusual cases and he was able to persuade the woman to talk frankly with him.

"I don't know where to start," began the woman. "A few weeks ago, when I went to the toilet, I started to hear *plunk, plunk, plunk*. When I looked in the bowl I noticed a pile of ten-pence pieces. After that it was twenty-pence pieces and now it's fifty-pence pieces. You don't believe me, do you?"

"Of course I do," said the gynaecologist. "This is quite normal. You're going through the change!"

MORE TOMMY

When I was in the scouts, the leader told me to pitch a tent. I couldn't find any pitch, so I used creosote.

Sometimes I drink my whisky neat.
Other times I take my tie off and leave my shirt out.

I'm on a whisky diet.
I've lost three days already.

I had a ploughman's lunch the other day. He wasn't happy.

Police arrested two kids yesterday. One was drinking battery acid and the other was eating fireworks.
They charged one and let the other off.

We were coming in to land and it affects your ears doesn't it?
The stewardess gave me chewing gum.
I put it in my ears. Took two days to get it out.

This little old lady was frightened. She looked at me and said, "Do something religious."
So I took up a collection.

My wife and I were fighting hammer and tongs.
She won. She had the hammer.

I bumped into an old acquaintance the other day. He told me he had just got a job as a postman. He said it was better than walking the streets.

I was cleaning the attic the other day with my wife.
Filthy dirty. But she's good with the kids.

I slept like a log last night. Woke up in the fireplace.

Our ice cream man was found lying on the floor of his van covered with hundreds and thousands.
Police say he topped himself.

I went to this energetic seafood disco the other night and pulled a mussel.

A man walks into a bar with a roll of tarmac under his arm and says, "Pint please—and one for the road."

A dyslexic man walks into a bra.

A sandwich walks into a bar. The barman says, "Sorry, we don't serve food in here."

A jump lead walks into a bar. The barman says, "I'll serve you. But don't start anything."

LUCKY CHARM

Bronwyn bought a lucky charm from a gypsy who told her that it would always give her what she wanted if she held it in her hand and counted 123. "BUT," warned the gypsy, "1234 must never be mentioned because it will lose its power."

150

Before attending, later that morning, a very important interview with the CEO of a big Company, Bronwyn had put it to the test and sure enough it had worked. So she was hoping that it would help her to land this well-paid job.

She nervously entered the interview room but her nerves disappeared when she took the charm from her purse, held it in her hand and muttered "123".

The CEO looked up and said, "What did you say 123 for?"

THE LUNCH BREAK

The same CEO later that day, took two of his female secretaries out for lunch and as the last drops of wine disappeared from the bottle, they were astounded when a genie appeared from the bottle and told them he would grant each of them a wish.

The first girl wished that she was on holiday lying on a sandy beach on a sunny island. The second girl wanted to be in Paris walking down the Champs Elysee.

"And what about you?" the genie asked the CEO.

The girls' faces dropped at his reply:

"I want them both back at their desks as soon as we've finished our meal."

KNOCK KNOCK
Who's there?
Opportunity.
Impossible. Opportunity only knocks once!

...& THE PAY RISE

One of the secretaries asked for a pay rise, saying that she enjoyed her job, but three companies were after her, so the CEO reluctantly agreed a 5% salary increase.

Afterwards, out of curiosity, he asked her who the three companies were who were after her.

"The electricity company, the telephone company and the rent company," was the reply.

OVERHEARD... in the school corridor

"Sir. Would you punish me for something I didn't do?"

"No Johnny, of course I wouldn't."

"Good Sir, because I haven't done my homework."

THE QUEEN'S RIDDLE

When Barack Obama paid a state visit to Britain, he asked the Queen how she managed to run such an efficient country.

"Surround yourself with intelligent people," was the Queen's advice.

"How do you know whether they are intelligent?" asked the President.

"I test them with a riddle," said the Queen. "I'll show you," she said, pressing a button on her intercom and asking for Tony Blair to join them.

"Yes, your Majesty?" said Tony as he entered the room.

"Would you answer this riddle for me, Mr Blair? Your mother and your father have a child. It's not your brother and it's not your sister. Who is it?"

"That would be me, your Majesty," replied the Prime Minister without hesitation.

"Yes. Very good," said the Queen.

When Obama went back to the White House he would put his close advisers to the test.

Calling in Joe Biden, he said, "Joe, I would like to ask you a question. Your mother and father have a child. It's not your brother or your sister. Who is it?"

"Not sure on that one, Mr President. I'll get back to you."

Biden asked several of the advisers but none could supply the answer until he met Paul Ryan in the Gym.

Paul came up with the answer right away. "That's me," he said.

"Good answer Paul," said Biden and hurried off to speak with the President.

"I've done some research on that riddle Mr President and I've come up with the answer. It's Paul Ryan."

The President was furious. He stomped over to Biden and yelled in his face:

"What kind of idiots do I have around me?" he fumed. "The correct answer is Tony Blair!"

...& THE QUEEN'S ADVICE

Kate Middleton asked her future mother-in-law for some advice on how to have a long and happy marriage.

"Wear a safety belt and don't piss me off," was Her Majesty's pearl of wisdom.

...& AGAIN

When Meghan complained to the Queen about getting heartburn every time she gave Harry oral sex. "Try Andrew's," suggested the Queen.

PRINCE CHARLES

The prince stopped off on his way to Balmoral to pay a visit to a hospital in Edinburgh, hoping to cheer up the patients.

He walks into one ward full of patients with no signs of illness or injury and speaks to one of the patients who replies:

"Fair fa your honest sonsie face'
Great chieftain of the puddin' race,
Aboon them a ye take yer place,
Painch, tripe or thairm,
As langs my arm."

Charles is confused by this reaction but just grins and moves
on to the next patient who responds to his greeting:

"Some hae meat and cannae eat,
And some would eat that want it,
But we hae meat an we can eat,
So let the Lord be thankit."

Even more bemused and his grin now rictus-like, he stoically
perseveres only to find the next patient chanting:

"Wee sleekit, cowerin, timrous beastie,
Oh the panic in thy breastie,
Tha needna start awa sae hastie,
Wi bickering brattle."

By now seriously confused and troubled, he turns to the
accompanying nurse and asks, "Is this a psychiatric ward?"

"Oh no," she replies. "It's a serious Burns unit."

**Pause for a moment and ponder, especially if you are one of
these people who knock our country. It's not perfect BUT
where else in the world could you poke fun like this at
heads of state and avoid imprisonment or worse?**

ON YOUR MARKS

A foreigner was shot in the head yesterday with a starting pistol.
The police believe it was race related.

QUIZ TIME

- How long did the 100-year war last?
- Where are panama hats made?
- What month do they celebrate the October revolution?
- What is a camel hair brush made of?
- The Canary Islands is named after which creature?
- What was King George VI's first name?
- What animal does cat gut come from?
- What colour is a purple finch?
- Where do Chinese gooseberries come from?
- What colour is an aeroplane's black box?

Answers later.

OVERHEARD... on 999

"Please help me. My wife is pregnant and her contractions are only 2 minutes apart."

"Is this her first child?"

"No. This is her husband."

THE HERMIT

"Wish You Were Here," a popular travel documentary in the 1970's, presented by Judith Chalmers, featured in one of its episodes a small fishing village in the West of Scotland. Miss Chalmers was particularly interested to interview a local hermit who had left to live high up in the mountains overlooking the village.

After a gruelling climb up the narrow path the camera crew eventually arrived at the hermit's tiny bothy.

At first he was reluctant to face the cameras but was persuaded to change his mind with a bottle of Glenlivet malt whisky.

Having heard whispers about this man by some of the villagers the first thing Miss Chalmers wanted to find out was why he had shunned the villagers and chosen to live in his lonely small bothy miles away.

"It's no me that did the shunning," said the hermit bitterly. "It's they ungrateful bastards doon there."

"Do ye see yon school hoose by the kirk doon there? Well I built that," he said. "But did they call me Hamish the school builder? Oh no."

"And ye see they wee cottages next to the school? Well, I built them as well. But did they call me Hamish the hoose builder? Oh no."

"And ye see the boats bobbin' around in the harbour? Well I built most of them too. But did they call me Hamish the boat builder? Oh no they didnae."

"Ye shag one lousy sheep…"

IRISH NEWS FLASH
Due to the recent water shortage Dublin swimming baths have closed lanes 7 and 8.

…& ANOTHER

The Irish have joined in the attack on Libya. They have sent in three ships—two full of sand and one of cement. It was a mortar attack.

QUIZ ANSWERS

- 116 years
- Ecuador
- November
- Squirrel fur
- Dogs
- Albert
- Horses
- Crimson
- New Zealand
- Orange

Thought it was easy eh? If you scored four out of ten, you're pretty smart.

THE COSTA CONCORDIA

In January 2012 this Italian passenger vessel foundered on rocks and 33 passengers perished, due in no small part, to the captain abandoning ship to save his own skin.
As often happens in such situations, after the news broke, the sick humourists were at work.

As the ship was sinking, one of the passengers rushed into the ship's cocktail bar and asked for a drink. "How would you like it sir?" asked the barman. "On the rocks," said the passenger.

"It's awful quiet on board," says Mick to his fellow passenger Paddy. "They'll all be listening to the band," replies Paddy. "I didn't realise that there was a ship's band," said Mick. "There must be," replied Paddy. "I just heard someone say a band on ship."

Winston Churchill was known to favour Italian cruise ships. Asked by a journalist for his reason, he replied:

"Three reasons. The first being the superb cuisine. Second, the excellent service and the third is that if there is a disaster there's none of this nonsense about women and children first."

POLLUTION?

Scientists, after many years of research into pollution, recently announced their findings.

"There are two things in the air," said a spokesman from the laboratory, "which we now know to cause women to become pregnant."

When questioned to be more specific, he announced, "Their left and right legs."

DAILY EXERCISE

A man told his wife that sex was healthy exercise.

"It's the equivalent of an eight-mile run," he claimed.

"Rubbish," replied his wife. "You can't run eight miles in twenty seconds."

OVERHEARD... at KFC

"May I take your order, sir?"

"Please tell me first, how do you prepare your chickens?"

"Nothing special sir. We just tell them straight away that they're going to die."

MY MAM plays war with me for sucking my thumb. You should see what she does to my dad.

SEX ON TV

Health and Safety have called for a ban on TV sex after a young couple Jason and Gemma Thompson were injured when the legs on the TV set gave way.

MOST MEN prefer looks to brains because they can see better than they can think.

MORE PARAPROSDOKIANS

I thought I wanted a career. Turns out I just wanted paycheques.

When I fill out a form, in the part that says "In the case of emergency please notify…" I put "A DOCTOR."

I didn't say it was your fault. I said I was blaming you.

A clear conscience is the sign of a fuzzy memory.

You don't need a parachute to sky dive. You only need a parachute to sky dive twice.

Money can't buy happiness but it makes living in misery easier.

I used to be indecisive. Now I'm not so sure.

You're never too old to learn something stupid.

To be sure of hitting the right target, shoot first and call whatever you hit, the target.

Change is inevitable—except from a vending machine.

I used to be a daydreamer but my mind kept wandering.

Religion is the main cause of conflict. Thank God I'm an atheist!

Work is the curse of the drinking class.

A bird in the hand makes it hard to climb a ladder.

It's not hard to meet expenses—they're everywhere.

He who laughs last thinks slowest.

I've had amnesia as long as I can remember.

BREAKING NEWS

After lying on the sea bed for 100 years, Irish divers were amazed to find that the Titanic's swimming pool was still full.

JAPANESE NEWS FLASH

The Japanese government today officially thanked Britain for the rescue dogs they sent out.
They said they were delicious.

PADDY'S DONKEY

Paddy bought a donkey from a farmer for 100 Euros.

The farmer said he would deliver the donkey the next day.

The next day he drove up and said, "I'm sorry Paddy, but the donkey's dead."

"Well just give me my money back," said Paddy,

"No can do," said the farmer. "It was alive when you bought it—and in any case, I've already spent it."

"Well just bring me the dead donkey," said Paddy. So the farmer brought him the dead donkey and asked Paddy what he intended to do with it.

"Raffle it off," said Paddy.

"You can't raffle a dead donkey," said the farmer.
"Sure I can," said Paddy. "Just watch me. I won't tell anyone it's dead."

A month later they met up again and the farmer asked Paddy what happened to the dead donkey.

"I sold 500 tickets at 2 Euros each and made a profit of 998 Euros," said Paddy.

"Didn't anyone complain?" asked the farmer.

"Just the guy who won," said Paddy. "So I gave him his 2 Euros back."

Paddy was head hunted by the Bank of Ireland and is now their investment director.

PADDY IN COURT

An Irish farmer, Paddy, was involved in a motor accident and was advised to claim damages for his injuries from the haulage firm whose lorry had caused the accident.

He was cross examined by the smart defence lawyer.

"Didn't you say to the police at the scene of the accident 'I'm fine'?"

Paddy responded: "Well I'll tell ya what happened. I'd just loaded my fav'rite cow Bessie into da...."

"I didn't ask for the detail," the lawyer interrupted. "Just answer the question. Did you not say to the policeman at the scene of the accident, when he asked you how you were, 'I'm fine'?"

"Well ya see," said Paddy, "I'd just got Bessie into da trailer, und was drivin' down the road..."

The lawyer interrupted again and said, "Your Honour, I am trying to establish the fact that, at the scene of the accident, this man told the police that he was fine. Now, many months later, he is trying to sue my client. I believe he is a fraud. Please tell him to simply answer the question."

By this time the judge was quite interested in what Paddy had to say about his favourite cow Bessie and asked Paddy to continue.

Paddy thanked the judge and proceeded. "Well, as I was sayin', I had just loaded Bessie into da trailer and was drivin' her down the road, when this massive truck came tunderin' tru a stop sign and hit me trailer right on da side. I was trown inta one ditch and Bessie was trown inta anudder. By Jaysus I was hurt, very bad like, und didn't want to move. But I could hear Bessie moanin' an groanin'. I knew she must be in terrible pain.

"Shortly after da accident a policeman on a motorbike turns up. He could hear Bessie moanin' an' groanin' too. So he went over to her and when he saw her condition he took out his gun and shot her right between the eyes.

"Den de policeman came over to me, with his gun still in his hand, and asked 'How are ya feelin'?'

"Now what da fuck would you say?"
Why can't other over sensitive people and cultures accept being the subject of humour and good-humoured ridicule like Paddy, his fellow countrymen and others?

ANOTHER (TRUE) COURT CASE (USA)

A lawyer from Charlotte in North Carolina bought a very rare and expensive box of cigars, then insured them against, among other things, fire.

Within a month, having smoked all of these expensive cigars, the lawyer filed a claim against the insurance company. In his claim the lawyer stated that they were "lost in a series of small fires."

The insurance company refused to pay, citing the obvious reason—that the cigars had been consumed in the normal way.

The lawyer sued—and WON.

Delivering the ruling the judge agreed with the insurance company that the claim was frivolous but, nevertheless, the lawyer had a policy with the insurance company in which they had contracted that the cigars were insurable and that it would insure them against fire, without defining what it considered would be "unacceptable fire." They were therefore obligated to pay the claim.

Rather than endure a lengthy and costly appeal process, the insurance company accepted the ruling and paid $1,500 to the lawyer for his loss of cigars which perished in the "fires."

After the lawyer had banked the money, the insurance company had him arrested on 24 counts of arson, using the lawyer's testimony from the court case against him.

The lawyer was convicted of the criminal offence of deliberately burning his insured property and was sentenced to 24 months imprisonment and a $24,000 fine.

This case won first prize in a 2015 USA Criminal Lawyers Award contest. It could only happen in America! Or could it? Britain's ambulance chasing legal rabble are catching up!

OVERHEARD... in confidence

"Dad, I shagged the girl next door last night."
"I hope you were careful and wore something."
"Yeah. A balaclava."

CENSUS FORM

Colin's census form was returned as unacceptable when, in response to the question "Do you have any dependents?" he answered, "2.1 million illegal immigrants, 1.1 million crack heads, 901 thousand people in 85 prisons and 650 idiots in parliament."

SUNDAY SCHOOL

A nun had just finished a lengthy explanation about dying and going to heaven.
She asked Suzy: "When you die and go to heaven, which part of you goes first?"

"I think it's your hands," said Suzy.

"Why do you think it's your hands Suzy?" said the nun.

Suzy replied: "Because when you pray you hold your hands together in front of you and God just takes your hands first."

"What a wonderful answer Suzy. Well done," said the nun.

Little Johnny then raised his hand and said, "Sister, I think it's your feet."

Puzzled, the nun said: "Whatever makes you think it's your feet Johnny?"

"Well," replied Johnny. "I walked past my mam and dad's bedroom the other night. Mam had her legs in the air and shouted out 'My God I'm coming' and if dad hadn't pinned her down I reckon we would have lost her."

ALZEIMERS & BRAIN TEST. (0NLY C3741N P30PL3 CAN R3AD 7H13)

7H15 M3554G3
53RV35 70 PR0V3
H0W 0UR M1ND3 C4N
D0 4MZ1NG 7H1NG5

1N 7H3 B3G1NN1NG
17 WA5 HARD BU7
N0W, 0N 7H15 L1N3
Y0UR M1ND 15
R34D1NG 17 4U70M471C4LLY
W17H0U7 3V3N 7H1NK1NG 4B0U7 17

I cdnuott blveiee that I cluod aulacity uesdnatnrd what I was rdanieg.

The phaonmneal pweor of the human mind, aoccdnig to a rscheearch dt Cmabrigde Uinevrtisy, it dseno't mtaetr in what oerdr the ltteres in a word are. The olny ipromtnt thing is that the frsit and last ltteer be in the rghit pclae. The rset can be a total mses and you can still raed it whotuit a pboerlm. This is bcusae the human mind deos not raed ervey lteter by istlef, but the word as a whole.

Azanmig huh?

And I awlyas tghuhot slpeling was ipmorrant.

GROWING OLD GRACEFULLY—Pam Ayres style

Will I have to be sexy at sixty?
Will I have to keep trying so hard?
Well I'm just going to slump

With my dowager's hump
And watch myself turn into lard.

I'm not going to keep exercising
I'm not going to take HRT
If a toy boy enquires
I'll say "hah, hard luck squire"
Where were you in '73?

I'm not going to shave my moustaches
I'm going to let them all sprout
My chins'l be double
All covered in stubble
I'm going to become an old trout.

My beauty all gone and forgotten
Vanished with never a quibble
I'll sit here and just
Kind of gnaw on a crust
And squint at the telly and dribble.

As my marbles get steadily fewer
Must I struggle to keep my allure?
Have I still got to pout
Now my teeth have come out
And my husband's found pastures newer?

Farewell to the fad and the fashion
Farewell to the young and the free!
My passion's expired!
At bed time I'm tired!
Sexy and sixty? Not me!

OVERHEARD... at the doctors

"Take these pills with two large glasses of water every two hours."
"Why, what's the matter with me?"
"You're dehydrated. You're not drinking enough water."

AGONY UNCLE GEORGE

Dear George.

Please can you help me.

A few days ago, shortly after leaving the house to go to work while my husband was watching TV, my car stalled and then broke down about a mile down the road and I had to walk back to get my husband's help.

When I got home I couldn't believe my eyes. He was in our bedroom with the neighbour's daughter.

I am 32 and my husband is 34 and the neighbour's daughter is 19. We have been married for 10 years.

When I confronted him he admitted that they had been having an affair for 6 months.

He has refused to go to counselling.
Shall I divorce him?

Sincerely, Sheila.

Dear Sheila.

A car stalling after being driven a short distance can be caused by a variety of faults with the engine.

Start by checking that there is no debris in the fuel line.

If it is clear, check the vacuum pipes and hoses on the intake manifold and also check all grounding wires.

If none of these approaches solve the problem it could be that the pump itself is faulty, causing low delivery pressure to the injectors.

I would strongly advise you to join one of the motoring organisations which offers roadside assistance.

I hope this helps.

George.

This is why men shouldn't do advice columns!

OUT OF THE MOUTHS OF BABES...

Now it's the turn of the young to have their say:

BABY TALK 1

DUDE
I'm JOKING you are NOT adopted !!!

THE SPEECH THERAPIST

An Englishman, a Scotsman and an Irishman attended a speech therapy session and the therapist promised to refund the fee if any of them could tell her, without stammering, the name of the town they originated from.

"B-B-B-B-B-B-B-irmingham," said the Englishman.

"P-P-P-P-P-P-P–aisley," said the Scotsman.

"London," said the Irishman.

"Well done," said the therapist as she handed him the £50 fee. "You can leave now. Goodbye."

As he walked through the door, he took a deep breath and blurted out, "…d-d-d-d-d-d-erry."

THE ENGLISHMAN... was later overheard to have the following conversation with a friend who asked him for his opinion on terrorism:

W w w w w well t t t t to t t t tell you the t t t t ttruth, I th th th th th think w w w w we should j j j j just d d d d d d drop a t t t t tomic b b b b b bombs on them and b b b b b blow them up t t t t t t too.

To which his friend replied, "It's easy for you to say that."

SANDWICH SHOP

Martin was surprised to see the final item on a list of sandwiches displayed outside a café: "Wanks £20."

Inside he saw a really attractive girl behind the counter. She greeted him with a smile and in a husky voice: "Good morning, I'm Lisa. What can I do for you today?"

"Are you the girl who does the wanking?" enquired Joe.

"I certainly am," said Lisa.

"Well," said Martin, "will you go and wash your hands and make me a cheese and tomato sandwich."

SHEIKH McABDULLAH

A wealthy Arab Sheikh during a visit to Scotland was suddenly taken ill and admitted to St Vincent Hospital in Glasgow where he was to undergo heart surgery. Unfortunately, he had a very rare blood type which resulted in a frantic search for a suitable donor.

When the operation was complete and the sheikh discovered that his life had been saved by the donor, he instructed his entourage for the donor to be rewarded with a new car and a gift of £5,000.

Unfortunately, the operation necessitated a second procedure and the donor's services were again called upon.

After this operation which was carried out entirely satisfactorily, the donor heard nothing. Expecting to be similarly rewarded he contacted the Sheikh to remind him that he expected his reward this time too.

"On yer bike," said the Sheikh. "I've got Scots blood in my veins now."

NEWSFLASH

The Irish government today announced that it had discovered a solution to their fuel shortage.

They have imported 50 million tonnes of sand from Saudi Arabia and will start drilling next week for their own oil.

FOREPLAY

FRENCH—Dinner, wine, sex.

ITALIAN—Dinner, wine, caressing, sex.

LATINO—Dinner, wine, dancing, caressing, sex.

SCOTTISH—"Haw ye awake?"

A PIPER'S LAMENT

I was once asked by a charity for the homeless, to play a lament at a funeral for an unfortunate old man who had died on the streets one cold winter's night. I would receive no fee but my heart was touched and I agreed.

Unfortunately, on the way to the graveyard I got hopelessly lost and when I arrived late the only people there were a group of diggers eating their lunch. I saw the hole in the ground had not been filled in so I went over and stood by it. I didn't know what to do so I started to play.

The workers put down their lunches and gathered round. It was a very solemn occasion and as I played "Amazing Grace" the workers were moved—some to tears.

Though my head hung low, my heart was full and as I walked away I heard one of the workers say, "I never seen nothin' like that before and I've been puttin' in septic tanks for twenty years."

I never found the proper place yet.

OVERHEARD... at the Vets

"I think my goldfish has epilepsy."

"It seems calm enough to me."

"Wait. I haven't taken it out of the bowl yet."

PADDY... at work

Paddy was doing some roofing work for Murphy.

As he reached the top of the ladder he started shaking and feeling dizzy.

He called down to Murphy: "I'll have to go home. I'm feeling giddy."

"Have you got vertigo?" asked Murphy.

"No," said Paddy. "I only live around the corner."

WOR LAD

When Geordie had a big win on the lottery his first thought was to give his son a good start in life, beginning with trying to improve his accent.

He took him down to the country's top elocution school in the south where he introduced his son to the principal and explained that, money no object, he wanted his son to talk proper: "Just like yea," he said.

"I will be delighted," said the principal in a posh plummy voice. "Just leave him with us for a couple of months then come to see us again and you will find a remarkable difference."

Geordie duly returned and asked the principal: "How's wor lad getten on like?"

"Please," replied the principal, "diven't yea tark tae me aboot your lad."

GEORDIE IN WALES

When his local pit closed down, Geordie moved to a Welsh mining village to find work.

Keen to make friends with the locals he got up bright and early on his first day and went for a walk.

"Good morning," he greeted the milkman who completely blanked him.

"Good morning," he cheerily bade the postman, who again ignored him.

The same thing with the butcher and the baker—and even the vicar.

On returning to his digs he asked his landlady why the locals were so unfriendly. She explained that it was a Welsh speaking village so they probably didn't understand him and that he should be greeting them with "Bore da sut wyt ti heddiw."

The following morning, despite the fact that it was freezing cold and pouring down, he resolved to try once more to make friends with the villagers and set off on his mission.

The first person he encountered was a BRS lorry driver stuck under his broken-down lorry, soaking wet and with oil dripping on him.

"Bore da...," began Geordie.

"Fuck off you Welsh bastard!" was the response.

BOBBY & THE BAILIFF

"Come in and take a seat, sir."

"I'm taking the lot."

BOBBY & THE BLITZ

"Get a move on Ethel, the air raid siren's gone."

"I can't find my teeth Bobby."

"They're dropping bombs, not pies," says Bobby.

Bobby Thompson was a 1940's North East comedian. Below are some gems from another North East comedian, Chubby Brown.

I got my girlfriend to smuggle my coke through customs by sticking it up her arse.
I didn't realise you could buy cans in the departure lounge.

The wife accused me of only wanting sex when I was drunk.
That's not true. Sometimes I want a kebab.

I was having a sneaky pee in the swimming pool and the lifeguard yelled at me so loudly, I nearly fell in.

There was a fat lass dancing on a table in the pub the other night.
"Good legs," I said.
She giggled and said, "Do you really think so?"
"Definitely," I said. "Most tables would have collapsed by now."

I think she fancied me 'cos she asked for my phone number.
I asked her if she had a pen and she said yes, so I said, "You'd better get back in it then, before the farmer misses you."

I told her I could tell which day a woman was born on by feeling her tits, so she let me have a go. After 5 minutes fondling, she said, "Go on then. What day was I born?"

"Yesterday," I said.

They're gonna make it more difficult to claim benefits. The claim forms are being printed in English.

My wife tried it doggy fashion, but she didn't like its smelly breath.

OVERHEARD... at the doctors (2)

"It hurts when I touch my leg. It hurts when I touch my head. It hurts when I touch my chest."

"Well it's bound to. That's a nasty gash you've got on your finger."

THE DEMON DRINK

Drink affects different people in different ways. It makes most people mellow and happy. But it makes others aggressive and sometimes violent.

The other night I went to the pub and had 8 pints of beer, leaving my wife at home drinking tea.

When I came in there were noisy scenes of abuse and violent physical assault.

I told her, If she can't handle her tea she should stop drinking it.

BABY TALK 2

CLEAN JOKE

Two brooms who had spent a long time hanging together in a closet finally decided they had enough in common to become permanent partners and got married.

The bride broom looked stunning in her wedding dress made from a multi coloured selection of dusters and the groom broom had his bristles cut and styled for the occasion.

At the reception the bride broom whispered into the groom broom's ear: "I think I'm going to have a baby broom."

"No, no, that's not possible," said the groom broom. "We haven't swept together yet!!"

LITTLE JOKE

A dwarf goes to a very good but very busy doctor and asks, "I know you are busy but do you treat dwarves?"

"Yes," replies the doctor, "but you'll have to be a little patient."

GENESIS 2:4—3:24

After 3 weeks in the Garden of Eden, God appeared before Eve. "So, how's everything going?" he asked.

"Oh, it's all so beautiful, God," she replied. "The sunrises and sunsets are breathtaking, the smells, the sights, everything... but there's just one small problem. It's the breasts you have given me. The middle one pushes the other two out and I am constantly knocking them with my arms, catching them on branches and snagging them on bushes. They're a real pain."

Eve went on to explain to God that since so many other parts of her body came in pairs—her limbs, eyes, ears and so on, maybe she should only have two breasts.

She told God that having only two breasts would, in her opinion, be much more comfortable and make her body more symmetrical.

"That's a very fair point," agreed God. "This is my first shot at creating a human. You can't always get things right at the first go. I gave animals six breasts, so I figured you would only need half of that. But you're absolutely right. I'll fix it right away."

And so God reached down and discarded the unwanted breast into the bushes.

God, three weeks later, again visited the Garden of Eden to see how things were.

"Well, Eve, how is my favourite creation?"

"Just fantastic," she replied, "but for one other oversight which I hope you won't take as a serious criticism."

"No, no," said God. "You've been very helpful. What can I do for you?"

"It's just that I noticed that all the animals are paired off. The ewe has her ram, the cow has her bull. They all have a mate except me. I feel so alone."

God thought for a moment and said, "You know Eve, you're right again. How could I have overlooked this? You do need a mate. Verily I say unto you I will right now create a mate from part of you. Now, let's see... where did I put that useless tit?"

GHOSTS

A professor at Wayne State University in Detroit was giving a lecture on Paranormal Studies and to get a feel for his audience, asked, "How many people believe in ghosts?"

About 90 students raised their hands.

"Well, that's a good start. Out of those who believe in ghosts, how many of you think you have actually seen one?"

About 40 students raised their hands.

"That's really good. I'm glad to see you taking this subject seriously. Has anyone actually touched a ghost?"

Four hands were raised.

"That's fantastic," said the lecturer and to lighten the subject he flippantly asked, "Has anyone made love to a ghost?" The laughter subsided as Hamad, sitting in the back row, raised his hand.

The professor took off his glasses and said, "Son, in all the years I've been giving this lecture, no one has ever claimed to have made love to a ghost. You've got to come out front and tell us about your experience."

The Middle Eastern student replied with a nod and a grin and began to make his way towards the podium. When he reached the front of the room the professor asked: "So, Hamad, tell us what it's like to have sex with a ghost."

Hamad replied: "Shit sir, from way back there I thought you said goats."

OVERHEARD... in intensive care

"Nurse, nurse, I can't feel my legs."
"Of course you can't. The surgeon's amputated both your arms."

QUICK THINKING

A man in Manchester walks into a Tesco supermarket and asks for half a lettuce.

"We only sell whole lettuces," says the young assistant.

The man gets stroppy and insists that the assistant consults his manager about this so the young boy walks into the manager's office and says, "Some stroppy bastard wants to buy half a lettuce."

As he finished his sentence, he turned around to find the man had followed him and was standing behind him, so he quickly added, "And this gentleman kindly offered to buy the other half."

Later, the manager praised the boy. "We like people like you who can handle themselves in awkward situations like that. You haven't been here long, have you? Where are you from?"

"New Zealand," said the boy.

"So why did you leave New Zealand?" enquired the manager.

"Sir," said the boy, "there's nothing but prostitutes and rugby players there."

"Is that right?" said the manager, glowering. "My wife's from New Zealand."

"Really," replied the boy. "Who did she play for?"

SCHOOL DISCIPLINE

A boy was sent home from school for swearing.

"I don't think that was clever," said his father sternly.

"No," said the boy, "it was c**t."

SECURITY USA STYLE

I took down my rebel flag (which you can't buy on ebay anymore) and peeled off the NRA sticker from my front door.

I disconnected my home alarm system and quit the candy-ass Neighbourhood Watch.

I bought two Pakistan flags and put one at each corner of my yard.

Then I purchased the black flag of ISIS (which you *can* buy on ebay) and put it in the centre of the yard.

Now the local police, sheriff, FBI, CIA, NSA Homeland Security and other agencies are all watching the house 24/7.

I've never felt safer—and I'm saving the $69.95 a month that ADT were charging me.

I bought burkas for my family for when we shop or travel. Everyone moves out of the way and security can't pat us down.

Safe at last—only in the USA.

OVERHEARD....in the gents.

"Does your wife let you have it doggy fashion?"

"No but we are into doggy tricks."

"Kinky, huh?"

"No not really. I kneel down and beg then she turns her back on me and plays dead."

ADVICE FOR NEW FATHERS

Q: How soon after she has given birth can you make love to your wife?

A: Depends whether she's in a private or public ward.

THE PREGNANT DAUGHTER

"I'll break every bone in the bastard's body!" screamed Linda Spencer's dad when he found out she was pregnant.

Linda was the apple of his eye. He was so intensely protective of his daughter. He got angry if a young man looked at her. Never mind this tragedy.

Eventually Linda persuaded her dad to meet the young man who had violated his daughter. When they met, Mr Spencer had to be restrained from setting about the young man.

"Please let me explain," pleaded the young man.

"I'll give you five bloody minutes!" said dad. "It had better be good."

"I love your daughter." said the young man. "I want to marry her. If it's a boy I will bequeath him my factory. If it's a girl I will bequeath her my villa in the Seychelles. And I will pay a dowry of £50,000."

"But what if I have a miscarriage dad?" said Linda.

"Well," replied Mr Spencer, "he'll just have to shag you again, won't he?"

EMU

An Aussie truckie walks into an outback café with a fully-grown emu behind him and orders a hamburger and a coke.

"Sounds great," says the emu. "I'll have the same."

"That will be $9.40," says the waitress.

The truckie reaches into his pocket, pulls out the exact money and pays.

The next day they come back. The truckie orders a hamburger and a coke and the emu says, "Sound great. I'll have the same."

The truckie again produces exactly the right money from his pocket and pays the bill.

This happens the next day and the day after that.

When they come back on the fifth day the waitress says, "Same again?"

"No, it's Friday, so I'll have a steak, baked potato and a salad."

"Sounds great," says the emu. "I'll have the same."

This time the bill was $36.70 and again the truckie pulls the exact money from his pocket.

The waitress could contain her curiosity no longer and asks the truckie how come he can instantly produce the exact money every time.

"Well love," explains the truckie, "last year I was cleaning out the back shed and came across an old lamp. I rubbed it and a genie appeared and offered me two wishes so I wished that if I ever had to pay for anything in the future, I could put my hand in my pocket and pull out the exact money."

"That's brilliant," said the waitress. "Most people would ask for a million dollars or something, but you'll always be as rich as you want for as long as you live."

"That's right," says the truckie. "Whether it's a pint of milk or a Rolls Royce, the exact money is always there."

Still curious the waitress asks, "So what's with the bloody emu?"

The truckie pauses, sighs and answers. "My second wish was for a tall bird with a big arse and long legs who agrees with everything I say."

MORE AUSSIE HUMOUR

Rachel, Claire and Samantha haven't seen each other since school. They rediscover each other via a reunion website and arrange to meet for lunch in a wine bar.

Rachel arrives first wearing an Alannah Hill outfit and orders a bottle of Pino Grigio and is shortly joined by Claire in a Sass &

Bide outfit. After the ritual kisses and hugs she joins Rachel in a glass of wine.

Then Samantha walks in wearing a faded old T-Shirt, jeans and boots and they all share another bottle of wine, after which they can't resist boasting about their lifestyles.

Rachel explains that after leaving Lauriston and graduating from Melbourne Uni Arts, she met and married Timothy with whom she has two beautiful daughters. Timothy is a partner at Mallesons. They live in a large house in Toorak where their daughters Charlotte and Emma take tennis lessons. They have a holiday house in Portsae and regularly ski in Canada.

Claire relates that she graduated from Monash Medicine and became an orthopaedic surgeon. Her husband Edward is a high-profile investment banker. They live in a Brighton beach front house and have a holiday flat in Little Cove, Noosa.

Samantha admits that she can't match that. She left school at 17 and ran off with her boyfriend Ben. They run a tropical park in the Byron Bay hinterland and grow their own vegetables. Determined not to be outdone by the others, she proudly tells them that Ben can stand 5 parrots side by side on his dick.

Half way down the third bottle of wine and several hours later, Rachel blurts out that her husband is actually only a bank teller at Commonwealth Bank, they live in a small house and have a caravan for their holidays at Tootgarook.

This shames and chastens Claire and, encouraged by her friend's honesty, confesses that she and Edward are both nurses' aides in a retirement home. They live in Rosanna and take holiday rips to Torquay.

Samantha admits that the fifth parrot has to stand on one leg!

OVERHEARD… in the changing room

"Did you find the shampoo?"

"Yes, but I'm not sure what to do with it?"

"Why not?"

"Well, it says it's for dry hair and I've just wet mine."

VIAGRA

"Last night I reached for my liquid Viagra and accidentally swigged from a bottle of Tippex. I woke up this morning with a huge correction!"

VIAGRA (2)

Grandpa and Grandma were visiting their kids overnight and Grandpa found a bottle of Viagra tablets in the medicine cabinet.

He asked his son if he could use one of the pills.

"I don't think you should take one, Dad. They're very strong and very expensive."

"How much?" asked grandpa. "£10 each," said the son.

"I don't care," said Grandpa. "I'll take one and leave the money under the pillow."

Later the following morning the son found £110 under the pillow and telephoned his dad to point out that he only owed £10.

"I know," said Grandpa "The other £100 is from your grandma."

VIAGRA (3)

Figures published recently by the British Medical Association have revealed that the money spent on research into Alzheimer's Disease is dwarfed by the amount spent on breast improvement surgery and Viagra.

According to one BMA spokesman, in fifty years' time there will be a large elderly population with pretty breasts, erect penises but with no recollection of what to do with them.

BOTOX

A sixty-five-year-old woman was so pleased with the result of her op she couldn't wait to hear what other people thought of her new looks.

"How old do you think I am?" she asked the newsagent.

"About 45?" he replied. "No, I'm actually 65!" she proudly announced.

She asked the same question with roughly the same response at the butchers, the florists and the off license.

But when she asked a man in the queue at the fish and chip shop he said "Sixty-five."

Deeply disappointed, she asked him why he thought she was so old.

"Because," he said, "I was behind you in the queue at the butchers."

OVERHEARD—in front of the mirror.

"Do you think I'm looking old? My breasts are sagging, my bottom's huge and my waistline has disappeared. I need a compliment from you to cheer me up. Do I look 58?"

"No you don't—but you did when you were!"

Q. Why do mothers dress their children in onesies?

A. Because they are too young to dress themselves!"

BEAUTY COMES FROM WITHIN

...within bottles, jars, make-up bags, jewellery boxes, hair sprays and perfume sprays!

DRINKS IN, WITS OUT

A group of friends having a quiet drink in a bar heard a thump and turned round to find one of the other customers lying on the floor, very, very drunk. They got him to his feet but he fell down again. He kept falling down every time they picked him up.

The friends decided to be good Samaritans and take him home. They asked him for his address but all they got was incomprehensible slurred gibberish.

Nobody knew where he lived so they searched his wallet and managed to find an address.

He fell down another three times before they got him into the car and again when they got him to his house.

"We brought your husband home," said one of the friends when his wife answered the doorbell.

"Where's his wheel chair?" asked the wife.

WABBITS

A little girl walks into a pet shop and asks, "Excuthe me, do you have any widdle wabbits?"

The shopkeeper kneels down beside her and says, "Do you want a widdle white wabbit or a thoft, fluffy bwack wabbit, or one like that widdle bwown one over there?"

The little girl blushes, rocks on her heels, leans forward and whispers, "I don't weally fink my pet pyfon gives a phuck."

GET OUT OF THAT

A butcher had almost sold out of chickens and was about to close shop for the weekend. There was only one left in the cold room. So he was delighted when a customer came in and asked to buy it.

The butcher weighed it and said, "That will be £4 please."

"Can I have a slightly bigger one?" asked the customer.

So the butcher took the chicken back into the cold room and emerged with the same chicken.

He put it on the scales, leaving his hand on the chicken to increase the indicated weight, hoping that would fool the customer.

It did—or at least he thought it did, because the customer said, "I'll take it thanks. In fact, I'll take them both."

...& THIS

On the eve of an important examination, three university students, instead of doing some last-minute revision, went out for a drink together. One thing led to another and in the early hours of the following morning they staggered out of a night club, returning to their lodgings at around 3am.

They were in no fit state to take the exam so, instead of doing so, they covered their shoes and trousers with mud and, an hour after the start of the exam, they went to the Dean's office and "explained" how, on the way to the college, one of the tyres on the car they were travelling in burst and the car swerved off the road and into a field.

They asked the Dean if, therefore, they could re-sit the exam.

Though suspicious, the Dean reluctantly agreed that they could do so three days later.

When the students arrived at the exam centre they were instructed to go into separate rooms where a question paper would be waiting for them.

There were only two questions on the paper—"What is your name?" was the first and the second was, "Which tyre on the car burst?"

TRUE LOVE

An old woman, sitting with her husband on the patio sipping a glass of wine, says, "I love you so much. I don't know how I could ever live without you."

"Is that you or the wine talking?" asks the husband.

"No," she replies, "It's me talking to the wine."

...& TRUE LUCK

An old man with very little going for him, after many years seeking, finally met a really good-looking young girl who fell in love with him—just two days after winning three million pounds on the lottery.

Talk about luck!

FACTS ?

£2.6 million home for Muslim family of 9 plus £90,000 annual benefits.

Former soldier Robert after 9 years front line service in Iraq now living with family in hostel.

£2 million home for Somalian family of 10 plus £100,000 home improvement grant.

£1.2 million home for single Afghan mother and 7 children plus £170,000 a year in benefits.

Soldier Michael after two tours in Afghanistan told by Council to live in homeless hostel with his family.

The sender of this email, Mr X, is saying, in effect, "If this is true then it's not fair."

Few would deny that the citizens of a civilised and wealthy country have a moral responsibility to set aside some of their wealth to help others who have been driven out of

their homes by no fault of their own and in circumstances beyond their control.

But it is the responsibility of the bureaucrats who are given the task of distributing this fund, to do so efficiently and intelligently and with regard to the sensitivities of the existing citizens. Failure to do so can have serious consequences.

It makes people like Mr X angry.

It creates an anti-immigrant culture and the emergence of extremist groups.

Spending such disproportionate amounts on individual families leaves less money in the fund to provide for other asylum seekers. It is not a bottomless pit!

It results in sophisticated and thriving people trafficking economies in poorer countries. The traffickers use examples like these to tempt their people to pay them large sums of money, which they may barely afford, to become illegal immigrants, many of whom die during perilous journeys before they reach the "promised land" or are refused asylum and sent back.

It results in more pressure on the resources of the host nation and poorer services for both immigrants and its indigenous people.

The culprits—those inept and unintelligent bureaucrats who administer the funding—those who should be made accountable for the rise in anti-immigrant feeling—neatly escape having to account for the consequences of their stupidity by labelling people who dare to question their incompetence, as racist, thus cleverly passing the buck.

OVERHEARD...over the garden fence

"Close your curtains next time you and your wife are having sex. The whole street was watching you and laughing at you yesterday."

"Well the joke is on you lot because I wasn't even home yesterday."

BANG

Paddy and his pal stole three grenades but had second thoughts and decided to take them to the police station and say that they found them.

"What if one explodes on the way there?" asked Paddy's pal.

"Well," said Paddy, "we'll tell them we only found two."

JETHRO'S TROUSERS

Every day, from morning till night, since he was a teenager, Jethro had suffered constant headache which had failed to respond to the various medication prescribed by his doctor.

In desperation he consulted a leading neurosurgeon who, after carrying out various tests, advised Jethro that the only cure for his problem was castration.

Jethro was at his wits end. His condition had had a massive effect on his quality of life, so he said to the surgeon, "Cut 'em off. I'll take them home for the dog."

Sure enough, this drastic measure did the trick. No more headaches for Jethro.

He had a new lease of life. He bought himself a new car and a new wardrobe of clothes, including a new top quality personally tailored suit.

Jethro was impressed when the tailor announced "You are a 44 chest and 30 inside leg" and wondered how the tailor could be so sure without even using his measuring tape. "Experience," explained the tailor. "I've been doing this for thirty years. You are also a 34 waist."

"No no," said Jethro. "I'm a 32. Have been for years." But the tailor insisted that 34 was correct. Again Jethro questioned the tailor's assertion.

The tailor shrugged his shoulders and said: "Okay. If you insist, I'll make the trousers 32 for you. But I warn you, they'll give you headaches!"

MAKE LOVE NOT WAR… or get married and do both!

WIFE: "I've changed my mind." HUSBAND: "Does the new one work?"

NEVER laugh at your wife's mistakes. You were one of them!

LAUGHING at your own mistakes lengthens your life. Laughing at your wife's shortens it.

THE IDEAL HUSBAND understands everything his wife doesn't say.

MARITAL RELATIONS

After yet another tiff, a couple sat in silence during a car journey until, as they were passing a field of pigs, the husband sarcastically remarked, "Relations of yours?"

"Yes," replied the wife—"In laws."

OVERHEARD—in the house (2)

"I had to marry you to realise how stupid you are."

"You should have known that the minute I asked you."

OVERHEARD—in the bedroom (2)

"Are you having sex behind my back?"

"Yes. Who did you think it was?"

SPERM COUNT

Anxious to discover why she couldn't get pregnant, a woman was advised by her doctor to bring a sample of her husband's sperm to the clinic.

They had little luck in trying to provide the sample.

The husband tried with one hand. He couldn't manage so he tried with two hands. The wife tried and she couldn't either.

He asked the lady next door to try.

None of them could get the lid off the specimen jar!

NEWSFLASH Australia

Police released 43-year-old Abdul Mazaan today following his arrest yesterday at Sydney airport under Australia's anti-terrorism laws when he was heard to shout "Hijack" causing panic among passengers waiting to board an Air Azira to Islamabad. His pal Jack Smith was able to corroborate his story that Abdul was simply saying hello to him.

MORE TOMMY

An airplane of spittle dived into the sea.
There were no salivas.

My tailor told me he was going to chop off the bottom of one of my trouser legs and put it in a library.
I thought, "That's a turn up for the books."

I'm very anti-hunting. In fact, I'm a saboteur. I go out the night before and shoot the fox.

So this bloke says to me: "Can I come in your house and talk about your carpets?"
I thought, "That's all I need, a Je-hoovers witness."

I told my mum that I was opening a theatre.
She said: "Are you having me on?"
I said, "Well, I'll give you an audition, but I'm not promising you anything."

Two fat blokes in a pub, one says to the other: "Your round."
The other says: "So are you, you fat bastard."

I was having dinner with Garry Kasporov the other night and there was a check tablecloth. It took him two hours to pass me the salt.
He told me that I reminded him of a pepper-pot.
I said: "I'll take that as a condiment."

I saw this bloke chatting up a cheetah. I thought, "He's trying to pull a fast one."

So I said to this train driver: "I want to go to Paris." He said: "Eurostar?" I said: "I've been on telly, but I'm no Dean Martin."

I said to this bloke in the pub: "Fancy a game of darts?"
He said: "OK then."
I said: "Nearest the bull starts."
He said: "Baa."
I said: "Moo."
He said: "You're closest."

Two cannibals eating a clown. One said to the other: "Does this taste funny to you?"

I went into a shop and said: "Can someone sell me a kettle?"
The assistant said, "Kenwood?"
I said, "Where is he then?"

I once met the bloke who invented crosswords. I can't remember his name. It's P something T something R.

I'm reading a really good book at the moment. It's called *The History of Glue*. I can't put it down.

I phoned the local ramblers club, but the bloke who answered just went on and on.

I went to Blackpool on holiday and knocked at the first boarding house I came to. A woman stuck her head out of an upstairs window and said, "What do you want?" I said, "I'd like to stay hear." She said, "OK then, stay there."

PAEDO

34 year old Amir booked a table at a posh restaurant for him and his 22 year old wife.

As they sat down, a group of people at the bar began chanting "Paedo, paedo"

It totally ruined their tenth anniversary dinner.

Just letting you know that the book,"<u>Understanding Women</u>" is now out in paperback

CRISIS IN THE VATICAN

There was consternation in the Vatican recently when the Pope had an erection and could not get rid of it. He was advised by his Cardinals that the only way to solve the problem was to have sex with a woman.

His Holiness immediately agreed but insisted on complete secrecy and three conditions.

The first condition, he said, was that she must not be a female of the Catholic faith.

The second condition was that her eyes must be blindfolded in case she recognised him.

"....and the third condition your Holiness?" enquired the Cardinals.

"She must have big tits and wear kinky boots."

TINGALING

Twelve Italian priests were being ordained and their vow of celibacy was to be tested. They were required to stand naked in two lines whilst two sexy naked girls danced provocatively before them. They each had a bell hanging on their penises to detect any unacceptable reaction. This was to be a test of their spiritual purity.

They all seemed to be passing the test successfully when the bell on Carlos who was in the front row began to ring violently. It fell off his penis on to the floor in front of him.

As he bent down to pick it up the other eleven bells rang like the clappers!

OVERHEARD—at a wedding

"Isn't the bride a right ugly dog?"

"Excuse me, that's my daughter you're talking about."

"Oh, I am sorry. I didn't realise you were her father."

"I'm not her father, I'm her mother."

"Oops!"

PHSYCHIATRIC ADVICE

Ever since I was a child, I've always had a fear of someone under my bed at night, so I went to a psychiatrist to see if he could solve the problem.

The psychiatrist suggested I should receive therapy every week and the problem would disappear after about a year.

"So how much does this therapy cost?" I enquired.

"£80 a session," he said.

Six months later I met him on the street and he asked me why I didn't go back to see him. "Decided to live with the problem, eh?" he said.

"No, it's sorted," I replied. "And it only cost ten quid."

"Come on," he said, "you couldn't get psychiatric advice that cheaply,"

"Didn't need it," I replied. "I mentioned it to a bloke in a bar who, for £10, told me to just saw the legs off the bed and I've had no problems since then."

SINGLES COLUMN AD

SINGLE BLACK FEMALE

Seeks male companionship. Ethnicity unimportant.
I am very good looking and I love to cuddle and play.
I like long walks in the woods, fishing trips and outdoor activities.
But I love the winter nights too, lying beside the fire and candlelit dinners will have me eating out of your hand.
I will be at the front door every night to welcome you, wearing only what nature gave me.
Ring ************ and ask for Daisy.

The 15,000 men who responded to this ad found themselves talking to the Atlanta RSPCA about a black Labrador retriever bitch!

THEY SAY a fool and his money are soon parted—but he can't be that daft or he wouldn't have got it in the first place.

BREAKING NEWS –Japan has announced their world cup squad:

1 膧楢琴执执
2 瑩泂牡楑砦执
3 执猥泂牡楑
4 敬瑉 瀰緹膧杢
5 执猥抙捡杣
6 淯渼 潤潭
7 昣咚咚慢正
9 敷止瑩札懒楤
10 淶楬皷牡氫晥
11 瑉戠瑝潴牻
12 浯潴 抳抳浩条
13 洷穡氭渑愭牧
14 揓敎琜琨灯抳
15 抳抳 慢正
16 牧畯挐桷愁皷
17 獭氭渑愭牧揓
18 敎琜琨灯
19 抳抳抳慢正
20 牧畯挐桷愁
21 皷楬皷牡 札散散汩
22 整 轴杯瀿
23 獽瑩溿皷
Coach: 楴敕执猥 搴筮

It's a mystery why they left 敎琜琨灯 out of the squad. He's world class.

BRAINS IN THEIR BOOTS?

"My parents have always been there for me. Ever since I was 7."
David Beckham

"I wouldn't be bothered if we lost every game. As long as we won the league."
Mark Viduka

"Alex Ferguson is the best manager I've ever had at this level.
Well, he's the only manager I've had at this level.
But he's the best manager I've ever had."
David Beckham

"If you don't believe you can win, there's no point in getting out of bed at the end of the day."
Neville Southall

"I've had 14 bookings this season—8 of which were my fault but 7 of which were disputable."
Paul Gascoigne

"Andy Ritchie has now scored 11 goals. Exactly double the number he scored last season."
Alan Parry

"I've never wanted to leave. I'm here for the rest of my life—and hopefully after that as well."
Alan Shearer

"I'd like to play for an Italian club like Barcelona."
Mark Draper

"You've got to believe that you're going to win and I believe we will win the World Cup until the final whistle blows and we're knocked out."
Peter Shilton

"I faxed a transfer request to the club at the beginning of the week, but let me state that I don't want to leave Leicester."
Stan Collymore

"I was watching the Blackburn game on TV on Sunday when it flashed on the screen that George (Ndah) had scored in the first minute at Birmingham. My first reaction was to ring him up. Then I remembered he was out there playing."
Ade Akinbiyi

"Without being too harsh on David Beckham, he cost us the match."
Ian Wright

"I'm as happy as I can be—but I have been happier."
Ugo Ehiogu

"Leeds is a great club and it has been my home for years, even though I live in Middlesbrough."
Jonathan Woodgate

"I can see the carrot at the end of the tunnel."
Stuart Pearce

"I took a whack on my left ankle, but something told me it was my right."
Lee Hendrie

"I couldn't settle in Italy—it was like living in a foreign country."
Ian Rush

"Germany is a very difficult team to play... they had eleven internationals out there today."
Steve Lomas

"I always put my right boot on first and then, obviously, my right sock."
Barry Venison

"I definitely want Brooklyn to be christened. But I don't know into what religion yet."
David Beckham

"The Brazilians were South American and the Ukrainians will be more European."
Phil Neville

"All that remains is for a few dots and commas to be crossed."
Mitchell Thomas

"One accusation you can't throw at me is that I've always done my best!"
Alan Shearer

"I'd rather play in front of a full house than an empty crowd."
Johnny Giles

"Sometimes in football you have to score goals."
Thierry Henry

"I've had bad luck with injuries, but I can't keep saying I've been injured a lot."
Jack Wilshire

"We haven't had the rub of the dice."
Bryan Robson.

FERNANDO

Fernando Torres walks into a bar and says, "I'll have two shots please!"
"That's not like you," said the barman

"You're through to PC World. How may I help you?"
"I'm having problems finding the net."
"Can I take your name please?"
"Fernando Torres."

THE NEW MANAGER

A new manager, desperate to succeed at his new club, persuaded the board of a newly promoted club, to give him millions of pounds to buy new players, assuring them that he would guarantee them three seasons in the Premier League.

His first signing was able to trap a ball further than most players could kick it. He defended the player, saying he was deceptive. "Don't worry, he's slower than he looks."

He was very popular with the female supporters who clamoured for his autograph—on their buttocks. They'd heard he was good at signing arseholes.

After the club was relegated after only one year in the top flight, he was hauled before the board and asked to explain himself.

"I kept my promise," said the manager. "We DID have three seasons in the Premier League—Autumn, Winter and Spring."

THE NEW SIGNING

Newcastle United were struggling when they signed the Brazilian star Mirandinha.

At his first team tactic talk the manager Willie McFaul drew a picture of a goal on the blackboard.

"This... Goal," he explained.

He then drew a picture of a ball and said, "This... ball."

Then a picture of a boot.

"This... boot." Then "Boot kick ball into goal."

"Please, Mr McFaul," interrupted Mirandinha. "I speaka da good English. You no need to explain this to me."

"I'm not talking to you," replied the manager. "I'm talking to the rest of the lads."

DICKS

In the nineties Arsenal had a player called David Dicks.

He suffered an injury and the local newspaper innocently carried a headline in the sports section "ARSENAL TO PLAY WITHOUT DICKS."

After receiving some objections, they hastily changed the headline in the later editions to "ARSENAL TO PLAY WITH DICKS OUT."

A record number of women turned out to watch the match.

WISHFUL THINKING

When Mackem Gerry was granted a wish by a fairy, he wished he could live forever, but when the fairy said that she was sorry because this wasn't included in her wish portfolio, Gerry said, "OK then. Can I live until Sunderland get back in the Premier League?"

"You smart bastard," said the fairy.

OVERHEARD.....in the outback

"I've forgotten how you throw a boomerang."

"Don't worry. It'll come back to you."

NEVER MARRY a tennis player.

To him love means nothing!

BABY TALK 5

THE BIG MATCH

As Spurs fan Simon took his seat in the South stand for the derby match against Arsenal, he was surprised to see a stranger in the next seat wearing Arsenal colours who explained that he was the brother of Gerry the season ticket holder, an ardent Spurs fan who hadn't missed a game for years.

"Where's Gerry today then?" Simon asked. "I'm surprised he's missing this big match. Where is he?"

"At home looking for his ticket," was the reply.

R.I.P

Steve and his wife had been season ticket holder in the Kop end for donkeys' years and never missed a game, so Jake, the fan in the adjoining seat, said to Steve that he was surprised to see her seat empty for such an important match against Man United.

"She died," explained Steve.

"Oh, I'm sorry to hear that. But seats are like gold dust today. Why didn't you give her ticket to one of your mates?" He was surprised at Steve's reply:

"They're all at the funeral."

K37

Bernie and Eric were season ticket holders at Old Trafford and were puzzled to see that the seat next to them—K37—was never occupied, particularly since these seats were in great demand.

So Eric made enquiries at the ticket office to see if they could buy the ticket for one of their pals, but he found that it had actually been sold.

Finally, someone occupied the seat for the Boxing Day fixture and they asked him why he hadn't been to any of the other matches.

"You wouldn't believe this," he explained. "My wife bought the season ticket in August for a surprise Christmas present."

PERVERT

Phone rings. Woman answers... pervert... heavy breathing. Voice says:
"Have you got a tight c**t?"

Reply: "Yes, he's watching the telly right now. Who shall I say is calling?"

SECURITY ALERTS

Global terrorism has resulted in a review of the levels of alerts used by several nations.

In England the level has been raised from "Miffed" to "Peeved". It seems likely that further action is needed and alert levels "Irritated" or even "A Bit Cross" may be necessary. The English have not been "A Bit Cross" since the Blitz of 1940 when tea supplies nearly ran out.

The Scots have raised their threat level from "Pissed Off" to "Let's Get the Bastards". They don't have any other levels.

Terrorists have been re-categorised from "Tiresome" to "A Bloody Nuisance". The last time this happened was in 1588 when threatened by the Spanish Armada.

The French government announced yesterday that it has raised its terror alert from "Run" to "Hide". The rise was precipitated by a recent fire at the French white flag factory, effectively paralysing the country's military capability.

Italy has increased its alert level from "Shout Loudly and Excitedly" to "Elaborate Military Posturing". A further level remains—"Change Sides".

The Germans have increased their alert state from "Disdainful Arrogance" to "Dress in Uniform and Sing Marching Songs". They also have two higher levels, "Invade a Neighbour" and "Lose".

Belgians on the other hand are all on holiday as usual. The only threat they are worried about is NATO and other headquarters pulling out of Brussels.

The Spanish are all excitedly looking forward to the deployment of their new submarines. These beautifully designed subs have glass bottoms so the new Spanish navy can get a really good look at the old Spanish navy.

Australia, meanwhile, has raised its security level from "No Worries" to "She'll be right, mate". Two more escalation levels remain—"Crikey, I think we may need to cancel the barbecue this weekend" and "Bloody Hell the barbie IS cancelled!"

OVERHEARD... in a prison cell:

"What do you think you're doing hanging from the ceiling by your feet?"

"I'm hanging myself."

"But the rope should be round your neck."

"I tried that but I couldn't breathe."

Q: Why do Scuba divers always fall backwards off the boat?

A: Because if they fell forward they would still be on the boat.

FOREIGN CALL CENTRES

I was so depressed last night thinking about the economy, wars. Global warming, my savings, Brexit, the government, my credit card debt. So I called the Samaritans. Their call centre was in Pakistan.

I told them about my problems and that I was feeling suicidal. They got excited and asked me if I could drive a truck.

ANOTHER RANT

This time by the Town Clerk of Dorval, a suburb of Quebec, Canada, who, following the mayor's refusal to remove pork from the menu of school dinners following demands by Muslim parents, issued the following statement entitled "PUT PORK ON YOUR FORK":

Muslims must understand that they have to adapt to Canada and Quebec, its customs, its traditions and its way of life. They must understand that it is for them to change their lifestyle, not the Canadians who so generously welcomed them.

Muslims must understand that Canadians are neither racist nor xenophobic. Canada accepted many immigrants before Muslims showed up, whereas the reverse is not the case, in that Muslim states do not accept non-Muslim immigrants.

Just like other nations, Canadians are not willing to give up their identity or their culture.

Finally, they must understand that in Canada, with its Judeo-Christian roots, Christmas trees, churches and religious festivals, religion must remain in the private domain.

The municipality of Dorval was right to refuse any concessions to Islam or Sharia.

For those Muslims who disagree with secularism and do not feel comfortable in Canada, there are 57 beautiful Muslim countries in the world, most of them underpopulated and ready to receive them with open halal arms in accordance with Sharia.

If you left your country for Canada and not for other Muslim countries, it must be because you considered that life is better in Canada than elsewhere. We will not let you drag Canada down to the level of those 57 countries.

Ask yourselves this question—just once. Why is it better here in Canada than where you came from? A canteen with pork on the menu is part of the answer.

If you came to Canada with the idea that you will displace us with your prolific propagation and eventually take over the country, you should pack up and go back to the country you came from. We have no room here for your ideology.

A similar proclamation was issued by Julia Gillard, the Prime Minister of Australia.

This controversial email was included in defence of free speech, with a plea to us all to adjust to the demands of integration. The Town Clerk's views may be applauded for their frankness by some and condemned as Islamophobic by others. Why not simply accept and respect them as someone's personal opinion, that's all?

Whatever your opinion is, in a diverse, free and democratic society we must never be afraid to express it and, if challenged, to justify it.

BACK SEAT DRIVER

This is a three-way conversation between a driver, a speed cop and the driver's wife in the back seat:

"I clocked you at 80 mph."

"I can't believe that. I put on the cruise control at 60."

"Now don't tell lies dear. You know we don't have cruise control."

"Sorry sir, I have to give you a ticket for speeding."

Why can't you keep your mouth shut? This will cost us £100."

"You should be thankful dear that the radar detector went off when it did, otherwise you would have been fined for that too."

"Didn't you know that radar detectors are illegal, sir? I'm afraid I will have to write out another ticket."

"I told you so dear."

"Will you just shut up, woman!"

"I notice also sir that you are not wearing your seat belt."
"No. I unfastened it to get my license out of my pocket when you stopped me."

"Now dear. You know you never wear your seat belt when you are driving."

"How many times do I have to tell you to button it?"

"I'm afraid that's another ticket sir."

"Now look what you've done, you silly bitch. This is going to cost me a bloody fortune."

"Does he always talk to you like this, madam?"

"No. only when he's been drinking!"

PROUD POSSESSION?

"You'll never have one of them," boasted little Johnny as he showed little Nancy his willy behind the bicycle sheds at school.

When Nancy told her mother about the incident her advice was to show her thingy to Johnny and just tell him that with that you can have as many willies as you want.

OVERHEARD—in Toxteth Liverpool

"Two quid to mind your car, sir?"

"No thanks, I leave my Alsatian dog in the back seat."

"Can he put fires out?"

NEWSFLASH Damascus.

Sheep farmer Abu Musab al-Zari appeared in court today accused of stealing livestock from a neighbouring Christian, Randi as Eli's farm.

The defendant denied the charge, claiming they were Islams!

BABY TALK 6

THE LOST WIFE (2)

A man approaches an attractive young lady in a supermarket and asks her if he can talk to her for a few minutes because he can't find his wife.

"How's that going to help you find her?" says the young woman.

"Because every time I've done that in the past, she appears in a flash out of nowhere."

INFIDELITY

The following week, the same man goes to the supermarket alone to give his wife a break from shopping.

He sees another attractive young lady there who he feels sure he had met somewhere before. So he goes up to her and says, "Excuse me, but have we met somewhere before?"

"Yes," replies the young lady. "You're the father of one of my kids."

His mind raced back to the only occasion he had been unfaithful to his wife.

"Are you the stripper at the bachelor party who I made love to on the pool table with all my mates cheering while your partner whipped my arse with wet celery?"

"No," came the frosty reply. "I'm your son's teacher."

OOPS!

The man's wife, a hospital worker, finished her shift early, came home and went straight upstairs where she saw four feet sticking out from the bed cover where there should only be two.

Furious, she grabbed a baseball bat, whacked the sleeping couple hard several times and ran sobbing downstairs and into the kitchen, where she found her husband reading the newspaper.

He greeted her with a "Hello love" and went on to explain that her parents had arrived unexpectedly and he had told them to sleep in their bed!

THE LOST BOY

A little Muslim boy had lost his mother in a supermarket and was being comforted by one of the customer service staff.

"What does she look like?" she asked.

"I don't know," sobbed the little boy.

HISTORIC ONE-SIDED BATTLES

In 1592 Edward the first of England decided to settle the Scottish problem once and for all.

His reconnaissance party had determined the location of the Scots on a steep brae and as Edward's 4,000 strong army approached, they were confronted by a lone ginger haired kilted five-foot-nothing Scot who yelled down at Edward: "Come up here ye English bastards and I'll gi' ye a hammerin!"

Edward turned to his commander and ordered him to dispatch ten men over the hill to deal with this upstart.

Twenty minutes later the little Scot reappears.

"Ye English diddies!" he yelled down. "Come on the rest o' ye, I'll take ye all on."

"Send 100 men!" ordered Edward. "This fellow must be taught a lesson."

Ten minutes later the Scot, a little dishevelled, appears again.

"Ye English scum!" he yells. "Y'ell no shut me up as easy as that."

Exasperated, Edward ordered 400 of his best men to wipe out the arrogant Scot.

Edward's commander, a little apprehensive by then, gulped and 400 men charged on horseback over the crest of the hill.

A few minutes later, covered in blood, the commander appeared at the top of the hill and yelled down: "Your Majesty, don't sacrifice any more men. It's a trap, there's two of them!"

OVERHEARD... in Killarney

"Christmas is on a Friday this year."

"Let's hope it's not the 13th."

NEWSFLASH SIAM

Suicidal sister kills twin by mistake.

PADDY saw a traffic warden writing out a ticket so he went over to him and said, "You nasty bastard. Have you got nothing better to do?"

So the traffic warden wrote out a second ticket for no road tax.

Paddy was furious and continued to give the traffic warden a hard time, so he wrote out a third ticket for bald tyres.

"It's your own fault," said a passer-by, "for being so abusive."

"I don't care," said Paddy. "It's not my car!"

HORSE SENSE is the thing that a horse has that stops it betting on humans.

HOW TO MAKE A SMALL FORTUNE AT THE RACES

Start off with a big one!

THE CENTIPEDE

Lonely and desperate for company an old man decided to get an unusual pet.

For reasons of economy he chose a centipede which would happily feed on leaves from wild plants.

The Sunday after getting his new pet he asked it if it would like to go to church with him.

The centipede didn't reply so the old man asked him again. Still no reply.

"I will ask you one last time," he said to his pet, "are you going to come to church with me?"

"I heard you the first time," said the centipede. "Give me a chance to put my shoes on."

THE GOOD OLD DAYS

When I was a kid my mother used to give me £1 to go to the shop and I used to come back with a loaf of bread, two bottles of milk, a dozen eggs, a piece of cheese and a bottle of whisky.

You can't do that these days. Too many fucking security cameras.

HARD TIMES

I come from a very poor family. It was tough. Particularly at Christmas time. If I didn't wake up with an erection, I would have nothing to play with.

(NOT SO DUMB) BLONDE

When so-called dumb blonde Rita died and arrived at the Pearly Gates, Peter was reluctant at first to let her in. Heaven was full of smart people and he was worried she wouldn't fit in.

"If you want to join us," said Peter, "you'll have to pass an intelligence test consisting of three questions."

"Fire away," said Rita.

"The first," said Peter, "is which two days of the week start with the letter T? The second question is, 'How many seconds are there in a year?' The third question is, 'What was the name of the swagman in the Australian song Waltzing Matilda?'

"You have 24 hours to come back to me with the answers," concluded Peter.

The next day Rita returned and with an air of confidence announced, "I've got the answers, they were easy."

St Peter raised his eyebrows and invited Rita to offer the answers.

"The first answer to the question how many days in the week begin with T is two—today and tomorrow."

Reluctantly Peter had no option other than to accept this answer, if only for its ingenuity.

"And the second answer?"

"Twelve."

Intrigued, St Peter said, "And how did you arrive at that number?"

"Second of January, second of February, second of March…"

"OK, OK," said St Peter, "that's enough. Can't really argue with that logic.

"And your third answer?"

"Andy."

"Andy?" said St Peter. "How on earth did you come up with an answer like that?"

"This was the easiest question," said the blonde.

"Explain please," said St Peter.

"Andy sat, Andy watched, Andy waited while his billy boiled," sang Rita.

"Come on in," said Peter with a broad grin on his face. "You'll cheer up the miserable lot I've got up here."

THREE DUMB BLONDES

Three blondes were interviewed for a vacancy in the Criminal Investigation Unit of the Metropolitan Police.

The Detective Constable conducting the interview stressed how important it was to recognise identifying features. He produced a picture of a man and asked each candidate to point out any distinguishing features.

"He's only got one eye," observed the first one, to which the slightly irritated interviewer responded by saying, "This is a profile picture. Of course you can only see one eye." She didn't get the job.

"He's only got one ear," observed the second candidate. She didn't get the job either.

"He wears contact lenses," announced the third candidate.

"How on earth did you reach that conclusion?" asked the interviewer.

"Well," she said, "he won't be able to wear glasses if he's only got one ear!"

She didn't get the job either.

BLIND FAITH

During the heavy floods in Calderdale on Boxing Day 2016 a flood warden advised an elderly couple to vacate their house which was situated in a particularly vulnerable location.

The couple refused to budge.

"Our faith is strong. We will rely on this to save us. God will protect us," they protested.

The water levels rose quickly and the authorities sent a fire engine to rescue them. Again, they refused the help, insisting that their faith in God would preserve them. They moved into an upstairs room when the ground floor became uninhabitable.

The floods intensified and a boat was sent to haul them out of the bedroom window.

They again insisted that God would protect them and as the flood levels rose they climbed on to the roof. So a helicopter was sent to save them. This too was rejected and the water eventually engulfed them and they perished.

They arrived at the Pearly Gates furious, demanding that Saint Peter summon God to explain himself.

When God arrived, they gave him a hard time. "We relied on our faith in you to save us!" they yelled. "Why did you do nothing to save us?" they demanded.

"Did bloody nothing?" said God, exasperated. "I sent a warden, a fire engine, a boat and a bloody helicopter, didn't I?"

God's greatest gift to us all is a mind of our own so that we do not need to accept blindly the preaching of others.

All religions promise their believers an afterlife existence.

Most religions, in their scriptures, promise and often describe, horrific everlasting punishment for sinners and non-believers in the afterlife. So why aren't those who profess to take their religious scriptures seriously, prepared to rely on God or Allah to carry out the prescribed punishments against the sinners and infidels?

Don't they trust their God or Allah? Do they think they can do a better job than God and Allah by themselves inflicting the punishments?

Will THEY themselves be punished for not trusting God/Allah to keep his promise to them?

OVERHEARD... outside Noah's Ark

"Did you enjoy the cruise?"

"No. It pissed down every day."

ON THE BUS

There was a young man from Darjeeling

Who got on the bus at Ealing

A note on the door said "DON'T SPIT ON THE FLOOR"

So he stood up and spat on the ceiling

Spike Milligan

BABY TALK 7

OVERHEARD... in church

"Our father, who does art in heaven,
Harold is his name."
(3-year-old boy)

CHURCH

Some go to church to see and be seen

Some go to church to say they've been

Some go to church to wink and nod

But few go there to worship God.

THE DESERT ISLAND

The Captain of a ship sailing past a desert island spots a man who has been stranded there for ten years, so the anchor is dropped and a boat sent to rescue the man.

"What are the three huts?" asks the Captain.

"The first one is my house and the second one is my church," replies the man.

"And the third?" enquires the Captain.

"Oh, that's the church I used to go to," replies the man.

OVERHEARD... in church (2)

"I've just done a silent fart. What shall I do?"

"Put some new batteries in your hearing aid."

OVERHEARD—outside the Pentecostal Hall

"How did the faith healing meeting go?"

"An absolute load of rubbish. Even the bloke in the wheelchair got up and walked out."

THE CAB

A devout Muslim gets into a taxi. He asks the driver to turn off the music, explaining that he must not listen because at the time of the prophet there was no Western music—the music of the infidel.

The cab driver politely switches off the radio, stops the cab and says:
"At the time of the prophet there were no taxis either, so please get out and wait for a camel."

Then he was hailed by three spotty youths. They thought it was an acne carriage!

After that he decided to pack in driving taxis. He was tired of people talking behind his back.

DANGEROUS IMPORTED FOODS

Attached to this email were some disturbing pictures of conditions under which some of the food which finishes up on our tables is treated and prepared.

Below are Bar Code numbers to watch out for. We make no recommendations. Use your own judgement. But remember that some foods which claim to have been produced in a place or country, may have only been packed there.

Europe Codes: 50 (UK), 30-37, 40-44, 57, 64, 76.
USA & Canada: 00-13.
China: 690-695.
Philippines: 480-489.
Australia: 93.
Taiwan: 471.
Middle East: 628-629.
Central America: 740-745.

Here is a selection of the undercover pics attached to this email. They depict a man on a motorbike collecting dead chickens and some of the environments where they are prepared before being sold on, presumably for export to restaurants or shops?

Make sure you are not the consumer!

ROAD SAFETY

"Wear something white at night," was the advice given by the AA to pedestrians.

So I did—and got knocked over by a snow plough!

THE HITCH HIKER

Driving along a country road I spotted a man with three eyes, no arms and one leg so I stopped the car.

"Eye, eye, eye," I said. "You look armless. Hop in."

UK GOVERNMENT ANNOUNCEMENT

Due to the current financial situation following the slowdown in the economy a scheme to retire people over 50 years old is being implemented. The scheme, Retire Aged People Early (RAPE) will be applied selectively.

Persons selected to be RAPED, if eligible, can apply to the government for the SHAFT scheme (Special Help After Forced Termination).

Persons who have been RAPED and SHAFTED will be reviewed under the SCREW programme (Scheme Covering Retired Early Workers). A person may be RAPED once, SHAFTED twice and SCREWED as many times as the government deems necessary.

Only persons who have been RAPED can get AIDS (Additional Income for Dependents and Spouse) or HERPES (Half Earnings for Retired Personnel Early Severance). Those persons who have had AIDS or HERPES will be able to apply and claim special status and excused being SHAFTED or SCREWED further.

Persons who are not RAPED and continue in employment will receive SHIT (Special High Intensity Training). The government prides itself on the amount of SHIT it provides.

Persons not receiving enough SHIT should contact their local MP who has much experience of providing this to constituents.

OVERHEARD... on the duck pond

"Quack, quack!"

"I'm going as quack as I can."

THE LAST KISS

A group of Pekin Illinois bikers were riding west on 1-74 when they saw a girl about to jump off the Murray Baker bridge.

The lead biker Richard stops, gets off his Harley, pushes through the crowd of gawkers, past the State Trooper who was trying to talk her down off the railing and says in a friendly voice: "Hey baby... watcha doin up there on that railin'?

"I'm going to commit suicide," was the tearful reply.

Richard didn't want to appear a softy, but he didn't want to miss this "be a legend" opportunity either, so he said, "Well, before you jump honey babe, why don't you give ole Richard here your best last kiss?"

To everyone's amazement she leaned back and did just that... and it was a long, deep lingering kiss followed by another equally intense one.

After they had breathlessly finished, Richard gets cheers from the onlookers and thumbs up approval from his biker buddies and even the State Trooper.

"Wow!" says Richard to the girl. "That was the best kiss I ever had honey. That's a real talent you're wasting, sugar shorts. You could be famous if you rode with me. Why the hell are you committing suicide?"

It wasn't clear whether she jumped or was pushed after her reply: "Because my parents don't approve of me dressing up as a girl."

COMMANDO INTERVIEW

Interviewer:
"We want a person with a suspicious mind, always alert, merciless, ready to attack at all times, acute sense of hearing, detective ability and most importantly someone with a killer instinct."

Applicant:
"Can my wife apply?"

B & Q's SHORTEST SERVING EMPLOYEE

When Alan retired he was lucky to find a job as a greeter at B & Q. After one hour his supervisor decided he was not cut out for this line of work and fired him. You will find out why when you read the following conversation with an unpleasant customer who walked into the store with her two children, yelling obscenities at them all the way through the entrance.

"Good morning. My name is Alan. Welcome to B & Q."

"Grunt."

"Nice kids you have there. Are they twins?"

"No. They're not fucking twins. The oldest one's nine and the other is seven."

"My mistake madam."

"Why the hell would you think they're twins? Are you blind or stupid, or both?"

"No madam. I am neither blind nor stupid. I just couldn't believe that someone would want to shag you twice."

A FRIEND OF MINE began dating a twin.

"How do you know you've got the right one?" I asked him.

"Easy," he said. "She's got tits and her brother has a dick."

PASSPORTS DOWN UNDER

This is a letter reported to have been sent to the Passport Office by an exasperated New Zealand citizen.

Dear Sirs.

I'm in the process of renewing my passport and still cannot believe this. How is it that Amazon have my address and telephone number and know that I bought a satellite dish from them back in 1997 and yet the government is still asking me where I was bloody born and on what date.

For Christ's sake, do you guys do this by hand? My birth date you have on my pension book and it is on all the income tax forms I've filed for the past 30 years. It is on my health card, my driving license, my car insurance, on the last eight bloody passports I've had, on all those stupid customs declaration forms I've had to fill in before being allowed to get off the dozens of planes I've flown on over the past 30 years and all those insufferable census forms.

Would somebody please take note, once and for all, that my mother's name is Mary Anne, my father's name is Robert and I'd be abso-fucking-lutely astounded if that ever changed between now and when I die!!!!!!!

I apologise for sounding off. I'm really pissed off this morning. Between you an' me, I've had enough of this bullshit. You sent the application form to my house—then you ask me for my fucking address!!!! What is going on? Do you have a gang of Neanderthal arse holes working there?

Look at my damn picture. Do I look like Bin Laden? I don't want to dig up Yasser Arafat for shit sakes. I just want to go and park my arse on some sandy beach somewhere. And would someone please tell me, why you would give a shit whether I plan on visiting a farm in the next 15 days? If I ever got the urge to do something weird to a chicken or a goat, believe you me, you'd be the last fucking people I'd want to tell.

Well, I have to go now, 'cause I've got to go to the other end of the poxy city to get another copy of my birth certificate to the tune of $60.

Would it be too complicated to have all the services in the same spot to assist in the issuance of a new passport the same day? Noooooooooooo, that'd be too damn easy and maybe make sense. You'd rather have us running all over the fuckin' place like chickens with our heads cut off, then have to find some arsehole to confirm that it's really me on the damn picture— you know, the one where we're not allowed to smile!!! Bureaucratic fuckin' morons. We couldn't smile if we wanted to, because we're all pissed off.

Signed
An Irate Citizen
Auckland

PS
Remember what I said about the picture and getting someone to confirm that it's me? Well my family have been in this country since 1776. I have served in the military and have had full security clearance, enabling me to undertake highly secretive missions all over the world. However, I now have to get someone "important" to verify who I am. You know, someone like my doctor—WHO WAS BORN AND RAISED IN FUCKING PAKISTAN!

CARDS

Bridge is like sex. If you don't have a good partner, you'd better have a good hand.

SPOTTED & OVERHEARD... in the park

Two men walking towards each other dragging their left feet behind them.

"What's the matter with your leg?" asks one of the men as they pass. "Old war wound. Normandy beach 1944," he replies, "and you?"

"Just trod on some dog shit"

MEALS ON WHEELS

THAT'S MY BOY

My son was thrown out of school today for asking a girl to give him a wank.
I said, "Son, that's three schools this year. You need to stop before you're banned from teaching altogether."

...& MINE

I was so proud of my boy when he told me that he had had sex with his teacher, that I went out and bought him a new bike. But he couldn't ride it straight away because he said his bum was still sore.

THAT'S MY BOY'S BOY

Last week I took my six-year-old grandson to a posh restaurant. I was so proud of the way he conducted himself.

He asked if he could say grace, bowed his head and recited: "God is good. God is great. Liberty and justice for all men... and I would thank you even more if I could have an ice cream for dessert."

Along with the laughter from nearby tables, a woman remarked loudly, "That's what's wrong with this country. Kids today don't even know how to pray. Fancy asking God for ice cream. Well, I never."

Hearing this my grandson burst into tears and asked me if he had done wrong and did I think that God would be mad at him.

I gave him a cuddle and reassured him that God was certainly not mad with him.

Just then an elderly gentleman approached our table, winked at my grandson and said, "I happen to know that God was most definitely *not* mad at you."

"Really?" said my grandson.

"Cross my heart," the man replied, and in a theatrical whisper, he added, "Too bad she never asks God for ice cream. A little ice cream is good for the soul. Don't worry about that grumpy old lady."

He then called over the waiter and ordered a huge sundae for the boy and when it arrived the gentleman, with a twinkle in his eye, said to the boy, "Now, what are you going to do with that then?"

The boy picked up his sundae, walked over and placed it in front of the woman and told her:
"Here. This is for you. Shove it up your arse, you grumpy old bitch."

3 PROUD DADS

It was Carnfield College's reunion and three old students were reminiscing when the subject of their children cropped up.

At this point one of the old friends excused himself to visit the bathroom, leaving the others to talk about their children.

"I've got a fine strapping son," said one. "He worked his way up from the bottom and is now chief executive of a national car distribution company. He earns so much money he bought a Mercedes for one of his friends last year."

"My son too is a fine young man," said the second old friend. "He too has been very successful in business. He is the head of a national real estate company and like your boy he too bought an expensive gift for a friend—an apartment in London."

At that point the third friend rejoined the company and was asked if he had any family.

"Yes," he replied, "but he's gay and works as a stripper in a night club."

The others began to sympathise but were interrupted as the third friend explained that he too was very proud of his son's achievements and how very popular he is, saying:

"In fact, one of his boyfriends bought him a brand-new Mercedes and another one bought him an apartment in London."

IRISH INGENUITY

An Irishman was granted three wishes by a Genie.

"Can I think about it for a couple of minutes?" he said.

After a couple of minutes he said, "Before I make my decision, I'd like to speak with my wife."

254

His wife immediately appeared out of nowhere and the Genie said, "Be careful now, that's two of your wishes used up."

"That was a bit stupid," remonstrated his wife. "You've only got one wish left now."

"Don't worry," he said. "My next wish is for three more Genies."

OVERHEARD—in the library

"Do you mind if I sit beside you?" **(quietly)**

"NO, I DO NOT WANT YOU TO HAVE SEX WITH ME." **(loudly)**

Stunned silence, then:

"I study philosophy so I know what a man is thinking. I know how to make people feel uncomfortable. I suppose you were embarrassed, eh?" **(quietly)**

"WHAT? £200 FOR JUST ONE NIGHT? WHO DO YOU THINK YOU ARE?" **(loudly)**

Stunned silence again followed quietly by:

"I study law and I know how to make people feel guilty." **(quietly)**

THE LAVATORY ATTENDANT

After forty-five years as a lavatory attendant at King's Cross station, old Joe finally retired.

He was presented with a watch at his leaving ceremony where his boss asked him how his final day at work had been.

"Well," said Joe, "all sorts of people use public toilets these days. One feller came in just to masturbate. Another came in with a young boy and locked himself in a cubicle. Then two men came in and performed oral sex on each other. Finally, someone came in for a shit. It was like a breath of fresh air."

BINGLE JELLS

CHRISTMAS CAKE RECIPE:

2 cups of flour
1 lb butter
1 cup of water
1tsp baking soda
1 cup sugar
1 tsp salt
1 cup of brown sugar
Lemon juice
2 cups of dried fruit
4 large eggs
Nuts
1 bottle of brandy

Sample the brandy to check quality
Take a large bowl and check the brandy again

Ensure the quality by pouring brandy in a cup and drinking it. Repeat.

Turn on the mixer and beat one cup of butter in the fluffy bowl. Add one teaspoon of sugar and beat again.

Before adding the brandy make absolutely certain of its quality by pouring into a cup and drinking it.

Turn off the mixery thingy.

Break 2 eggs and chuck in the bowl with the dried fruit.

Pick the fruit up off the floor.

Mix off the turner.

Use a screwdriver to pry off any fried druit stuck to the beaters.

Check the brandy for concisticity.

Next, sift 2 cups of salt—or something.

Check the brandy.

Now shift the lemon juice and strain your nuts.

Add one table and a spoon of sugar—or whatever you can find.

Greash the oven.

Turn the cake mix 360 degrees and try not to fall over.

Don't forget to beat off the turner.

Finally, throw the bowl through the window, finish the brandy and wipe the counter with the cat.

...AND A CHRISTMAS TRADITION EXPLAINED

When four of Santa's elves called in sick, the trainee elves could not produce toys as quickly as the regular ones. It was Christmas eve and time was running out.

Santa's mood wasn't improved when Mrs Claus announced that her mother was coming to stay over Christmas.

He then discovered that two of the reindeers were due to give birth and refused to get into harness.

One of the harnesses came loose which frightened the other reindeers, causing one of them to bolt.

In trying to stop it, one of the toy sacks fell off the sleigh and toys were strewn all over the road.

Santa, totally stressed out by this time, needed a drink so he went back indoors to pour himself a cup of apple cider and a shot of rum, only to find that the bottle was empty because the elves had drunk it all.

The cup slipped out of his hand and smashed into dozens of pieces all over the kitchen floor.

When he went to fetch a broom to clear up the mess, he found that the mice had chewed away all the bristles.

Just then the doorbell rang.

He went to the door and yanked it open.

There on the doorstep was a sweet little angel.

She greeted him with a "Merry Christmas Santa. I've brought you a present." She showed Santa the beautiful Christmas tree and asked him where she should stick it.

You've guessed the rest.

And so was born the tradition of the fairy on the Christmas tree.

VIRUS WARNING

Beware of a dangerous virus which can cause your social life to crash.

It is known as the Worry-Overload-Recreational-Killer (WORK).

If it comes in the form of unpaid HOUSEWORK you are recommended to purchase one of the antidotes Bothersome-Employer-Elimination-Rebooter (BEER) or Work-Isolating-Neutraliser-Extract (WINE).

You are advised to take care since they are known to have side effects. These include:

Causing you to tell your friends over and over again that you love them.

Causing you to believe that you can sing.

Causing you to think that you can converse enthusiastically with members of the opposite sex without spitting.

Causing you to believe that you are whispering when you are actually shouting.

Creating the illusion that you are tougher, smarter, faster and better looking than most people.

DUST IF YOU MUST

Dust if you must, but wouldn't it be better
To paint a picture or write a letter,
Bake a cake, or plant a seed;
Ponder the difference 'tween want and need?

Dust if you must, but there's not much time,
With rivers to swim and mountains to climb;
Music to hear and books to read:
Friends to cherish and a life to lead.

Dust if you must, but the world's out there
With the sun in your eyes and wind in your hair;
A flutter of snow, a shower of rain.
This day will never come round again.

Dust if you must, but bear in mind,
When old age comes, it won't be kind.
And when you go (as go you must)
You yourself will make more dust!

GLORY

At a dinner in his honour during the Napoleonic wars, the great man Bonaparte was asked if he deserved the glory for his victories.

"Should not some of the credit be given to all those officers and soldiers who fought face to face with the enemy on the front line?" asked one of the guests.

"I would be delighted," replied Napoleon, "for them to take *all* the glory, *all* the credit, if like me, they will take the blame when we are defeated."

STARBUCKS

I was in Starbucks yesterday when, suddenly, I became desperate for a fart. The music was really loud so I timed my farts with the beat to disguise them.

After a couple of songs I finished my latte feeling much better.

I wondered why everyone was glaring at me. Then realised I was listening to the music on my iPad.

THE LOVE DRESS

A woman stopped by unannounced at her son's house one day, knocked at the door and walked straight in to find her daughter-in-law lying on the couch wearing nothing but expensive perfume.

"What on earth are you doing?" she asked the girl.

"I'm waiting for Mike to come home from work," she replied. "This is my love dress."

"But you're naked!" exclaimed her mother-in-law.

"Mike loves me to wear this dress," she explained. "It excites him no end. Every time he sees me in this dress he instantly becomes romantic and makes passionate love to me for hours on end. He can't get enough of me."

When the mother-in-law got home she undressed, showered, put on her best perfume, dimmed the lights, put on a romantic CD and lay on the couch waiting for her husband to arrive.

He finally arrived, saw his wife lying there provocatively and said, "What the hell are you doing?"

"This is my love dress," she whispered sensually.

"Needs ironing," he said. "What's for dinner?"

He didn't get any more dinners for the next six months.

OVERHEARD... at the greengrocers

"A pound of carrots please."

"It's kilos now."

"OK, I'll have a pound of kilos then."

SNOTTY RECEPTIONIST

A man had an appointment with a urologist who shared a reception desk with other doctors.

He approached the receptionist with trepidation. She was a severe, unfriendly looking woman and when the man gave her his name, she totally embarrassed the man by announcing in a booming voice:

"Yes, I have your name. You want to see the doctor about impotence, right?"

The others in the waiting room turned to have a look at this poor chap, who retrieved the situation with this brilliant riposte:

"No, I've come to enquire about a sex change, but I don't want the doctor who did yours!"

DARREN

The compiler is assured by Steve Springer, a Tenerife bar owner, that this is a true story about his pal Darren, an

exceptionally talented all-round sportsman who decided he would take up golf. He bought a new golf bag, a set of top of the range clubs and all the gear, at a cost approaching £2,000. Darren had always been able to quickly achieve proficiency in every sport he played. Until, that is, he tried golf.

Steve and five friends, including Darren, were playing Los Lagos golf course in Tenerife. Steve was in the first three ball and Darren in the following one. Darren appeared to be having a torrid time.

Standing on the 7th tee Steve saw Darren hit two balls into the lake adjoining the 6th fairway. Darren walked towards the lake, then lifted his golf bag and clubs above his head, hurled them into the water and stormed off back towards the club house.

The other five were surprised and a bit disappointed that Darren had apparently had enough of golf. Then, a few minutes later they saw Darren again walking towards the lake. This time he didn't stop, but carried on walking into the water and retrieved his clubs.

Their first reaction was one of relief and approval that Darren may have had second thoughts and decided to persevere with the game after investing so much money in it.

Their next reaction was one of wide-eyed disbelief when Darren once again lifted his bag and clubs above his head and threw them back into the lake, again storming off towards the club house.

Later, when they caught up with Darren in Steve's bar, they were intrigued to find out what on earth was going on earlier.

"What the hell," asked Steve, "were you doing going back to retrieve your clubs from the lake, only to immediately throw them back in?"

"I'd left my car keys in one of the bag pockets," explained Darren.

And so the mystery was solved.

Darren stuck to football, tennis and snooker from then on.

NYMPHOMANIAC CONVENTION

A man boarded an aircraft at Heathrow bound for New York. As he settled into his seat, he noticed a beautiful woman boarding. There was a spare seat beside him and he quietly hoped that she would occupy it.

His wish came true as she reached up to place her hand luggage overhead enabling him to appreciate her stunning figure. His heart skipped a beat as she slid into the seat beside him.

"Hello!" he blurted out. "Business trip or vacation?"

She turned, smiled enchantingly and said, "Business. I'm going to the annual Nymphomaniac Convention in the United States."

He swallowed hard. Here was the most gorgeous woman he'd ever seen sitting next to him—and she was going to a meeting for nymphomaniacs!

Struggling to maintain his composure, he calmly asked, "What's your business role at this convention?"

"Lecturer," she responded. "I use my experience to disprove some of the popular myths about sexuality."

"Really?" he smiled. "What myths are those?"

"Well," she explained. "One popular myth is that African-American men are the most well-endowed, when, in fact, it's the native American Indian who is the most likely to possess that trait.

"Another popular myth," she went on, "is that Frenchmen are the best lovers, when, actually, it is men of Greek descent."

The man listened intently, his mind working feverishly as she continued:

"We have also found that potentially the best lovers in all categories are the Irish."

Suddenly the woman became uncomfortable and blushed.

"I'm sorry," she said. "I really shouldn't be discussing this with you. I don't even know your name."

"Tonto," the man said. "Tonto Papadopoulos. But my friends call me Paddy."

OVERHEARD on the beach:

"My wife is such an ungrateful bitch."

"Why's that?"

"This year when I arranged our annual holiday, I chose Skegness for her and her mother, but she thought the caravan I booked for her was too small. So I arranged B & B at a boarding house just ten minutes' walk from the beach. She complained about having to go out to buy a meal at night. So I arranged B & B and evening meal inclusive. She still wasn't happy. She wanted to come to the Five Star hotel in the Seychelles with me!"

THE SHOE SALESMAN

A leading shoe manufacturer in the UK wanted to get into exporting so he advertised for a salesman.

"I want you to go to Africa," he told the first interview candidate, "and sell our shoes over there."

"But they don't wear shoes in Africa," complained the candidate.

He didn't get the job. But the second candidate did.

When the same proposition was put to him, he replied, "What a terrific opportunity. All those potential customers!"

MORE TOMMY

A man went to see a psychiatrist wearing only cling film. "Well," said the shrink, "I can clearly see your nuts."

Two blondes walk into a building... you'd think at least one of them would have seen it.

Answering machine message:
"If you are calling to buy marijuana, please press the hash key."

I went to buy some camouflage trousers the other day but I couldn't find any.

I went into the butchers the other day and bet him fifty quid he couldn't reach the meat off the top shelf. He refused. He said the steaks were too high.

My friend drowned in a bowl of Muesli. A strong currant pulled him in.

I went to a seafood disco last week and pulled a mussel.

Two eskimos in a kayak in sub-zero temperature decided to light a fire on the craft to keep warm. It sank, proving once and for all you can't have your kayak and heat it.

Our ice cream man was found lying on the floor of his van covered in hundreds and thousands. Police say that he topped himself.

A man takes his cross-eyed Alsatian to the vet and asks if there is anything that can be done about it. The vet picks up the dog and examines its eyes, then checks its teeth. Finally, he says:
"I'm going to have to put him down."
"What?" says the man. "Just because he's cross-eyed?"
"No. Because he's heavy."

So I rang up British Telecom and said, "I want to report a nuisance caller." They said, "Not you again."

I bought my wife a wooden leg for Christmas. It wasn't her main present—just a stocking filler.

I bumped into an old friend today.
He's got poor eyesight as well.

DUCKS IN HEAVEN

Three female friends died simultaneously in a car crash. On their arrival in heaven they were surprised to see swarms of ducks all over the place. Saint Peter warned them that it was very important not to tread on one, which was very difficult to do because they were all over the place.

It wasn't long before one of the new arrivals stepped on a duck.

Along came Saint Peter with the ugliest man she had ever seen.

"Your punishment," announced Peter, "is to be chained to this man for eternity."

Despite taking great care, it wasn't long before the second woman stood on a duck and was duly given the same punishment.

This made the third woman very wary and for several months she was able to avoid the punishment. But to her amazement she sees Saint Peter walking towards her with the most handsome man she had ever clapped eyes on.

She was even more amazed when she was strapped to this beautiful hunk. Although puzzled, since she had not stood on a duck, she raised no objection.

A little while later the couple started chatting and the woman mentioned the fact that she was surprised to find herself in this situation.

"I didn't even stand on a duck," she told him.

"I did," replied the man.

THE PAPAL CHAUFFEUR

The Pope was bored being driven around in his limo so he decided one day to swap places and drive himself.

He enjoyed the freedom so much he floored the accelerator pedal and reached 150 kph on the road out of Rome, chased by a motor cycle speed cop.

When he eventually pulled over and the cop realised who it was, he didn't know what he should do, so he telephoned his chief, explaining that the speeding motorist was a VIP.

"All the more reason to book him," said the chief.

"But he's really, really important," said the cop.

"Who is it, the bloody mayor?" asked the chief.

"No, even more important," said the cop.

"Not the bloody president surely?" asked the chief.

"No. Even more important than the President," said the cop.

"Impossible," said the chief. "Who the hell is it then?"

"I think it's God," said the cop.

"God?" exclaimed the chief. "What on earth makes you think it's God?

"Well," said the cop. "He's got the Pope as a chauffeur."

SLEEPOVER

"Are you still a virgin?" Richard asked his school pal Tony after his sleepover at Richard's house.

"I was till last night," said Tony.

"You're lying," said Richard. "We stayed indoors all night."

"Ask your sister," said Tony.

"I don't have a sister," said Richard.

"You will in nine months," said Tony.

ALICE

My name is Alice Smith.

As I was sitting in the waiting room at the dentists, I recognised the name on the dentist's diploma on the wall.

Could this be the same David Fraser? The tall handsome, dark haired boy who was in my class at secondary school? Could this be the same boy I had a secret crush on all those years ago?

But when I was eventually called through for my treatment, I immediately thought "No". This balding, grey haired, wrinkled old man was surely too old to have been my classmate.

Nevertheless, my curiosity prompted me to ask him if he was the same David Fraser who was a pupil of the Morgan Park Secondary School thirty years ago.

"Yes, I was. I was indeed an old Morganian," he beamed with pride. "Why do you ask?"

"Because you were in my class!" I exclaimed. "Do you remember me?"

Then the ugly old fat-arsed bastard said, "What subject did you teach?"

OVERHEARD... in Merthyr Tydfil

"Gwyneth Jones is getting married."

"Is she pregnant?"

"No, she's not pregnant."

"Well now, there's swank for you."

GREECE

My son wanted to know what it was like to live in Greece.
So I stopped his pocket money.

VEGETARIAN ANIMAL LOVER Tracey thought she had met her ideal man when her date told her he worked with animals—until she discovered later that he was a butcher.

GRAVY TRAIN

A small rural town in Spain twinned with a similar town in Greece.

The mayor of the Greek town visited his counterpart in Spain and was impressed by the Spanish mayor's palatial house. And wondered how he could afford such a house.

The Spaniard pointed out of the window and said, "Do you see that bridge over there? The EU gave us a grant to build a two-lane access between the two hills so I only built one way and put traffic lights at each end."

The Greek mayor was very impressed and extended an invitation for the Spaniard to visit him the following year.

When he did, he found the Greek mayor's house to be even more splendid than his own and was interested to discover how this had been achieved.

The Greek mayor asked the Spaniard, "Do you see that bridge over there?"

The reply?

"No?"

18th CENTURY NURSERY RHYME
(Substitute corrupt politicians for lords and ladies)

They hang the man and flog the woman
Who steals the goose from off the common
Yet let the greater villain loose
That steals the common from the goose.

The law demands that we atone
When we take things we do not own
But leaves the lords and ladies fine
Who take things that are yours and mine.

BREXIT

Many of our ancestors, the Chartists, the Suffragettes, Suffragists and others, endured ridicule, hardship and some sacrificed their lives so that ordinary people could have a direct say, through the ballot box, in who should make the laws we must all obey.

This fundamental inalienable right was diminished when Britain's trade agreement with Europe was allowed to escalate into a political alliance in which unelected bureaucrats in Brussels were given license to decide what we may or may not do or believe.

Whatever the merits of a common market are, many people decided that these were not worth preserving if, in return, we must surrender what was achieved by the sacrifices of those heroic martyrs two centuries ago. This is why many people, in the referendum of 2016, voted to leave Europe.

It was a close vote and what swung it perhaps, was the content of a leaked document from EU headquarters which revealed their intention to break another promise to the British government. This was that the EU would adopt English and not German as the common European language—Eurospeak.

We can reveal here the contents of that document.

ARTICLE 364/12, Section 138, sub section 23—Cultural Changes.

PROPOSED CHANGES TO BYE LAW 105 ARTICLE 364/12

In consideration of the British government's concession that some improvements could be made to the spelling of some words in the English language, the following changes will be phased in over a period of five years:

In the first year the soft "C" is to be replaced by "S".
Sertainly this will make it easier for the sivil servants in Brussels to embrase the change.
The hard "C" will be dropped in favour of "K".
This should klear up konfusion and keyboards kan have one less letter.

We anticipate growing publik enthusiasm in the sekond year when the troublesome "PH" will be replaced by "F" this making words like fotgraf 20% shorter.

In the third year publik akseptanse of the new spelling kan be expected to reach the stage where more komplikated changes are introduced.

Governments will encourage the removal of double letters which have always been a deterent to akurate speling.
Also, al wil agre that the horibl mes of the silent "E" in the language is disgrasful and it should abandond.

By yer four, people will be reseptiv to steps such as replasing "TH" with "Z" and "W" with "V".

During ze fifz yer, ze unesesary "O" kan be dropd from vords containing "OU" and after ziz fifz yer, ve vil hav a reil sensibl riten styl.

Zer vil be no mor trubl or difikultis and evrivun vil find it ezi tu understand ech oza. Ze drem of a united urop vil finali kum tru.

Und efter ze fifz yer, ve vil al be speking German like zey vunted uz to do in ze forst plas.

THE GRAND OLD DUKE OF YORK

He had ten thousand men,

He also had some young girls.

But he can't remember them.

BREAKING NEWS

New Brexit negotiator appointed

NEWSFLASH—Brexit

The result of the second referendum were announced today.
Remain won by a tiny majority.
They are going to do best out of three next year.

POLITICS versus the PEOPLE

51.9% - PEOPLE who voted Brexit

75% - REGIONS who voted Brexit

60% - LABOUR CONSTITUENCIES who voted Brexit

70% - CONSERVATIVE CONSTITUENCIES who voted Brexit

27% - MPs who voted Brexit

BREXIT—THE BMA's VIEW

A survey of Britain's physicians was taken recently but it failed to achieve a consensus.

The Allergists were in favour of scratching it, but the Dermatologists advised not to make any rash moves.

The Gastroenterologists had a sort of gut feeling about it, but the Neurologists thought Mrs May had a lot of nerve.

Obstetricians felt certain that everyone was labouring under a misconception, while the Ophthalmologists considered the idea short sighted.

The Pathologists were the most vocal group, chanting their slogan "Over my dead Body" which irritated the Paediatricians who advised them to "Grow up".

The Psychiatrists thought the whole idea was madness, while the Radiologists claimed they could see right through it!

Surgeons decided to wash their hands of the whole affair and the Internists agreed that it would be a bitter pill to swallow.

The Plastic Surgeons opined that the proposal would "put a whole new face on the matter."

The Podiatrists thought it was a step forward, but the Urologists were pissed off at the whole idea.

Anaesthesiologists thought the whole idea was a gas, and those lofty Cardiologists didn't have the heart to say no.

In the end the Proctologists summed it up, saying, "Those arseholes in Parliament are not interested in our opinions. They just want to hang on to power or use it all as an excuse to have a general election."

But a spokesman for the Colorectal surgeons disagreed, accusing the Proctologists of "Talking shit."

THE KNOWLEDGE

Before being allowed to drive a black cab in London, drivers must pass a test known as "The Knowledge"

The examination is considered to be one of the most demanding in the world, often requiring years of study to manoeuvre the city's 25,000 labyrinthine streets and landmarks.

To everyone's surprise, dyslexic Colin passed with flying colours.

Asked afterwards if he had found it tough, Colin replied "Not really. It was as easy as C A B!"

UK ANNOUNCES NEW 50P COIN TO COMMEMORATE BREXIT

The next few pages of this book will probably appeal more to the older generation and the final pages "Laughter on the Links" to golfers, but most people will, hopefully, enjoy the humour, philosophy and pearls of wisdom which follow. We will all be old one day!

THE TWILIGHT YEARS

There comes a time in your life when you realise:
Who matters.
Who never did.
Who won't any more.
….and who always will.

So don't worry about people from the past. There's a reason why they didn't make it into your future.

The irony of life is that by the time you are old enough to know your way around, you're not going anywhere!

You were always taught to respect your elders but it gets harder and harder to find any.

DONALD & ROSE

92-year-old Donald and his wife Rose had invited their old friends round for dinner and while the girls were in the kitchen, Donald was enthusing about the bar meal he had earlier in the week.

"Who did you go with?" asked the friend.

Donald went to the kitchen door and shouted through to his wife, "Darling, what was the name of that pub we went to the other night?"

"The Rose and Crown," replied his wife.

"Oh, I remember now," said Donald to his friend, "I went with Rose."

The following morning Donald asks Rose to go and make him a cup of tea. Ten minutes later she comes back with a sandwich. An exasperated Donald snaps at her: "Where are my eggs?"

They finished up in the same old people's home.

"Can you hear me?" said Donald to Rose. He repeated the question twice again, each time louder than the previous time.

Turning to the Matron, he said, "She's going deaf." Then he shouts at the top of his voice "CAN YOU HEAR ME?"

The Matron writes a note and gives it to Donald. It says: "Rose has replied four times to your question, saying YES SHE CAN HEAR YOU!"

OVERHEARD... in the care home

"Are you alright Ethel? You've been standing on those stairs for twenty minutes."

"Am I going up or coming down?"

DAMMIT I'M MAD

…is dammit I'm mad spelt backwards.

AGE & WEALTH

With old age comes riches:

Silver in the hair.
Gold in the teeth.
Crystals in the kidneys
Iron in the arteries
Sugar in the blood
…and an inexhaustible supply of gas!

BEFORE YOU DIE

Unless you want to give your family members hours of frustration, remember to cancel your credit card before you die.

The following telephone conversation between a deceased's family member and a customer service person of XXXX Bank was reported in the *Newcastle Evening Chronicle*:

"I am calling because you have sent my mother a letter to say you have applied an annual service charge to my mother's credit card. She died in January."

"The account was never closed, so late fees and charges still apply."

"Maybe you should turn it over to debt collectors as it says in your last letter."

"We already have. It is now two months overdue."

"So what will they do when they find out she's dead?"

"Either report her account to the frauds division or report her to the credit bureau."

"Do you think God will be angry with her?"

"Excuse me?"

"Did you get what I was telling you? The bit about her being dead?"

"Sir, you will have to speak to my supervisor."

"Hello sir. I am the supervisor. The account was never closed. The late payment fees will still apply."

"You mean you want to collect it from her estate?"

"Are you her lawyer?"

"No. I'm her grandson."

"Could you fax us a certificate of death?"

"Sure."

"Our system isn't set up for death. I don't know what I can do to help."

"Well, if you figure it out, fine. If not just keep billing her. I don't think she will care. She doesn't live there anymore."

"Well. The late fees still apply."

"Would you like me to give you her new address?"

"That would help."

"Heaton Cemetery. Heaton Road. Newcastle upon Tyne. Plot 1049.

"Sir. That's a cemetery"

"Well what the xxxx do you do with dead people on your planet?"

XXXX Bank were not available for comment when a reporter from the *Evening Chronicle* rang.

WHO'S NEXT?

Was this the same old lady who had left instructions that after her funeral service, the wreath should be removed from the coffin and thrown into the crowd to see who would be next?

OVERHEARD....in the old folks' home:

"I'm 83 today and I'm really struggling with aches and pains. How about you?"

"I'm nearly 90 and I feel like a new born babe – no hair, no teeth....and I've just wet my pants!"

Apparently there's a third option between burial and cremation.

RETIREMENT SPEECH

At Albert's retirement 'do' his boss gave the following speech:

"Today I would like to recognise and thank Albert for his 40 years of loyal service to the Company. He has been a dedicated servant. Albert has never refused hard work. He doesn't know the meaning of tea break, or impossible task, or lunch break, or finishing early—so today I have much pleasure in presenting him with this Oxford Concise Dictionary!"

OVERHEARD.......at the airport.

This case weighs a ton. What have you put in it, the kitchen sink?"

"No. But I wish I'd brought the kitchen table."

"Why's that?"

"Because I left the tickets on it."

NOSTALGIA isn't what it used to be!

Here are a few memories which may astound the younger generation.

Many of us hadn't seen a TV set until we were in our teens—and then in black and white.

Programmes ended at 10pm with The Epilogue to remind us that we were in a Christian country, followed by the National Anthem.

Even though we were poor we were proud of our country and its heritage in those days.

You were never driven to school. The only person with a car was the local doctor.

Some kids were lucky enough to have bikes—but not many.

Bikes were the most common form of transport—and you had to wear trouser clips to stop the oil from the bicycle's chain dirtying your trousers.

The only telephones in your town or village were in the police station—and police stations were always within walking distance.

Later on, when telephones became more widely available—and affordable—you had to share it with a party line.

All mail was first class.

Pizzas were unheard of. They certainly weren't delivered to your home—but milk was—by an early morning milkman from his milk float.

So were newspapers. All newspapers were delivered by newspaper boys and most boys delivered newspapers to teach them a work ethic.

Film stars kissed with their mouths shut. At least they did in their films—and there was no profanity or graphic violence or sex. You had to use your imaginations. People had imaginations in those days!

There were no "Seniors" just OAPs (Old Age Pensioners).

Families used to eat at a table together at the same time.

When you'd finished your meal you asked for permission to leave the table.

Eating out meant tea at your gran's.

Rationing and ration books—you were allowed one egg per week.

If you didn't get into the team because you weren't good enough, that was that.

Mona Kitty and other "dangerous" school playground games were great fun—and very competitive. So were conkers and alleys.

No washing machines or spin driers. Just scrubbing boards and mangles.

No central heating. Just coal fires and fenders and a shovel with a newspaper over it to blast air into the grate—after you'd thrown sugar on the coal!

Toasting forks held over the flames (no electric toasters then).

Rag and bone men with a horse and cart collecting unwanted anything.

Grocers' shops sold things loose in paper bags not in hermetically sealed containers, because nobody had ever thought about poisoning a perfect stranger.

Loose tea leaves in paper bags from tea chests.

Brown tea pots, knitted tea cosies and tea strainers.

Taking drugs meant having your polio injection.

Race issue meant who could run the fastest.

Having a weapon at school meant being caught with a water pistol, a catapult or a spud gun.

It was bad luck if you didn't sit down and count to ten when you went back to collect something you'd forgotten.

....and remember that old BT advert for telephones, "It's good to talk"? It worked and years later we all bought smart phones to communicate without speaking!

NOSTALGIA USA STYLE

Long ago and far away in a land that time forgot,
Before the days of Dylan, or the dawn of Camelot,
There lived a race of innocents and they were you and me,
For Ike was in the White House in that land where we were born.
Where navels were for oranges and Peyton Place was porn.
We longed for love and romance and waited for our prince.
Eddie Fisher married Liz and no-one's seen him since.
We danced to Little Darlin' and sang to Stagger Lee,
And cried for Buddy Holly in the land that made me, me.
Only girls wore earrings then—and 3 was one too many,
And only boys wore flat top cuts, except for Jean McKinney.
And only in our wildest dreams did we expect to see,
A boy named George in lipstick in the land that made me, me.
We fell for Frankie Avalon, Annette was oh so nice,
And when they made a movie, they never made it twice.
We didn't have Psycho Five, or Star Trek Two and Three,
Or Rocky Rambo Twenty in the land that made me, me.
Miss Kitty had a heart of gold and Chester had a limp,
And Reagan was a Democrat, whose co-star was a chimp.
We had a Mr Wizard but not a Mr T,
And Oprah couldn't talk yet in the land that made me, me.
We had our share of heroes. We never thought they'd go.

At least not Bobby Darren, or Marilyn Monroe.
For youth was still eternal and life was yet to be,
And Elvis was forever in the land that made me, me.
We'd never seen the rock band that was grateful to be dead,
And airplanes weren't named Jefferson and Zeppelins were not Led.
And Beatles lived in gardens, and Monkees lived in trees,
Madonna was Mary in the land that made me, me.
We'd never heard of microwaves, or telephones in cars,
And babies might be bottle fed, but they weren't grown in jars,
And pumping iron got wrinkles out and gay meant fancy free,
And dorms were never co-Ed in the land that made me, me.
We'd never seen enough of jets to talk about the lag,
And microchips were what was left in the bottom of the bag.
And hardware was a bag of nails and bytes came from a flea,
And rocket ships were fiction in the land that made me, me.
Buicks came with portholes and side shows came with freaks,
And bathing suits came big enough to cover both your cheeks,
And Coke came just in bottles and skirts below the knee,
And Castro came to power in the land that made me, me.
We had no Crest with fluoride. We had no Hill Street Blues.
We had no patterned pantie hose, or Lipton Herbal Tea,
Or prime time ads for those dysfunctions in the land that made me, me.
There were no golden arches, or Perrier to chill,
And fish were not called Wanda and cats were not called Bill,
And middle age was 35 and old was forty-three,
And ancient were our parents in the land that made me, me.
But all things have a season, or so we hear them say,
And now instead of Maybelline we swear by Retin-A.
They send us invitations to join AARP.
We've come a long way baby in the land that made me, me.
So now we face the brave new world in slightly larger jeans,
And wonder why they use smaller print in glossy magazines.

And we tell our children of the way it used to be.
Long ago and far away in the land that made me, me.

THE £2.99 SPECIAL

An old couple went into a café.

"Two eggs, bacon, hash browns, beans and toast for £2.99. That is very good value," said the wife to the waitress. The rest of the conversation went like this:

"Yes madam. It's our £2.99 Seniors Special breakfast."

"Sounds good—but I don't want the eggs."

"In that case madam it will be £3.49."

"That's ridiculous. So you say I have to pay extra for not taking the eggs?"

"I'm sorry madam but if you don't stick to the set menu we have to charge you a la carte."

"Okay, then I will have the eggs."

"How would you like your eggs madam?"

"Raw and still in their shells."

So that is how they were served.

She took the eggs home with her and used them to bake a cake.

Old folk learn to be thrifty!

MARGARET'S 40th BIRTHDAY PARTY

"What kind of presents are these?" fumed Margaret. "A children's comic, white ankle socks and a sherbet dip? ....and what's that bloody clown doing here?"

"But," said her crestfallen husband, "when I asked you what you would really like for your birthday you said you'd like to be six again."

"You idiot," she fumed, "I meant my dress size."

YOUNG WIVES

"How's your new lovely young wife?" enquired the vicar when he called at 80-year-old Silas's farm one day.

"I can't keep my hands off her," says Silas.

"That's good I suppose," said the vicar.

"Not really," said Silas. "She's run off with one of them."

So when Silas's neighbour, 77-year-old Joe married a woman 50 years younger than him, Silas advised him to take in a lodger.

A year later Silas asked his neighbour how things were working out. "Great," said Joe. "My wife's pregnant."

"I knew it!" said Silas. "So has she run off with the lodger?"

"No, no," said Joe. "She's pregnant too."

Most people will know the tale of the old bull and the young bull where the young bull says "Look, dad, look. The farmer's left the gate to the cows' field open. Let's dash in and mount one." "No, son," says the old bull "let's take our time and mount them all."

Here is a doggy version:

THE OLD DOG

An old Doberman was chasing rabbits and became so intent on his task that he found himself in unfamiliar surroundings. Wandering about, he notices a hungry young panther heading towards him menacingly.

The old dog had to think quickly and noticing some old bones on the ground he settles down to chew on them with his back to the panther and just as the panther was about to pounce the old dog licked his lips and said, "Mmm, that was one delicious panther. I wonder if there are any more around here."

The young panther stops in his tracks with a look of terror on his face and slinks away into the trees.

"Whew!" exclaimed the panther. "That was a close shave. The old Doberman nearly had me."

Meanwhile, a squirrel who had been watching from a nearby tree, figures he can put his knowledge to good use and trade it for protection from the panther so he sets off after the panther, spills the beans and does a deal with the panther.

The young panther is furious at being made a fool of by the dog. "Hop on my back," he says to the squirrel. "Wait and see what I am going to do with that conniving canine."

When the Doberman sees the panther approaching again with no fear and a menacing look in his eyes, his preservation instinct again kicks in and again has to think quickly.

Realising that, fast as he is, he is no match for a panther, he again turns his back on the panther and pretending not to have seen him, exclaims loudly, "Where's that squirrel? I sent him off an hour ago to bring me another panther."

The furious panther has squirrel instead of dog for his lunch!

The moral of this story is that you shouldn't mess with old dogs. Age will always overcome youth and treachery. Bullshit and brilliance only come with age and experience!

Q. What do you call a dog with no legs?

A. It doesn't matter. He won't come anyway!

SECOND BEST

I had always suspected, and was finally convinced, that my twin brother was her favourite when my mother asked me to arrange the candles on the cake for his surprise birthday party!

**Guide Dog for a Muslim Woman . . .
they call it a BARKA**

ONE FINAL RANT

It's hilarious all these school kids preaching to us that we fucked up the planet. When I was a kid there wasn't a plastic bottle in sight. All bottles were glass and we took them back to the shopkeeper who used to give us a refund, or money off the next bottle of pop. The bottles were washed and re-used. No plastic bags either. Vegetables were weighed and put directly into a linen shopping bag or a basket. In my day we walked to and from school. Mummy didn't pick us up in her 4+4. No fast food takeaways except fish and chips and they were wrapped in old newspapers. No polystyrene food boxes to litter the streets. Our milk was delivered each morning in bottles by a milkman who drove an electric vehicle! Holidays were in Britain at B&Bs or in caravans. No jetting off to far away destinations. So I think these youngsters should take a look in a recycled mirror, reflect on this and think is it my generation or there's which is the problem.

ANOTHER ALZEIMERS TEST

You have 15 seconds to fill in the blank spaces to complete the words.

```
_ _ NDOM
F _ _ K
P _ N _ S
PU _ S _
S _ X
BOO _ S
```

Answers: RANDOM, FORK, PANTS, PULSE, SIX, BOOKS

You got all six wrong, didn't you? But don't worry, you haven't got Alzheimer's—but you *are* a pervert.

HEREDITY

If your parents don't have any children, neither will you.

TECHNOLOGY

Most oldies either ignore technology or struggle with it.

Those who do make the effort to use emails discover that there is a virus which only seems to affect the over 65s. These are the symptoms:

1.   Causes you to send the same email twice.
2.   Causes you to send a blank email.
3.   Causes you to send an email to the wrong person.

4.	Causes you to send it back to the person who sent it to you
5.	Causes you to forget to attach the ATTACHMENT.
6.	Causes you to hit "Send" before you are finished.
7.	Causes you to hit "Delete" instead of "Send"
8.	Causes you to "Send" when you should "Delete"

It's called the C-NILE VIRUS. Even the most advanced and sophisticated programmes from Norton to McAfee have failed to find a solution.

Hmmm… have I sent this to you already? Or did you just send it to me?

TECHNICAL SUPPORT

Of course there's always the technical support teams to talk you through your problems. Here are a few examples of conversations between customers and technical support staff:

"Hello. How can I help you?"
"I can't print."
"Will you press on 'START' for me and…
"Listen pal. Don't get technical with me. I'm no Bill Gates."

"I have problems printing in red."
"Do you have a colour printer?"
"Aaaaah… thank you."

"I can't get on the internet."
"Are you sure you have entered the correct password?"
"Yes. I'm sure. I saw my co-worker do it."

"Can you tell me what the password was?"
"Yes, it was six dots."

"Good afternoon. This is Martha. I can't print. Every time I try, it says 'CAN'T FIND PRINTER'. I even lifted the printer and put it in front of the monitor and it still couldn't find it."

"What kind of computer do you have?"
"A white one."

"My keyboard is not working any more."
"Are you sure it is plugged into your computer?"
"No. I can't get behind the computer."
"Pick up the keyboard and take ten steps backwards."
"Okay."
"Did the keyboard come with you?"
"Yes."
"That means your keyboard is not plugged in."

"What's on your keyboard now madam?"
"A teddy bear that my boyfriend bought me at the 7-11 store."

GETTING AWAY WITH IT

Because they are old we often get away with things we wouldn't have done when we were younger. This next story epitomises this.

An elderly couple were celebrating their sixtieth anniversary. They had married as childhood sweethearts and had moved back to their old neighbourhood after they retired.

Holding hands, they were walking past their old school and for sentimental reasons went inside and asked the head if they could find the old desk on which Andy had carved "I love you Sally". The kindly head readily agreed.

On their way back home a bag of money fell from an armoured car. They picked it up and took it home. Andy wanted to take it to the police station but Sally thought it should be a case of "finders' keepers" so after counting out the money—fifty thousand dollars—they put it in the bag and hid it in the attic.

The next day there was a knock on the door and Sally answered it and found two police officers there. They were canvassing the neighbourhood looking for the money.

"Pardon me," said one of the officers. "Did either of you find a bag of money that fell out of an armoured car yesterday?"

"No," lied Sally.

"She's telling lies," said Andy.

"Don't believe him," said Sally. "He's getting senile."

The officers turned to Andy and began to question him. One said, "Tell us the story from the beginning."

"Well," said Andy, "when we were walking back from school yesterday..."

The first police officer turned to his partner and said, "Come on, we're wasting our time. Let's get outa here."

Andy and Sally had a lovely holiday in the Bahamas that year.

WINE FOR SENIORS

A new wine which guarantees a good night's sleep has been developed in the Hunter Valley region, famous for its production of the Pino Noir, Pino Grigio and Pino Blanc wines.

They have developed a new grape which acts as an anti-diuretic which they claim reduces nocturnal toilet visits dramatically.

They've called it the Pino More!

FIFTY SHADES OF GREY HAIR

The missus bought a paperback
Down Dimmocks Saturday,
I had a look inside her bag
T'was Fifty Shades of Grey.

Well, I just left her to it,
At ten I went to bed.
An hour later she appeared,
The sight filled me with dread...

In her left hand she held a rope,
And in her right a whip.
She threw them down upon the floor
And then began to strip.

Well, fifty years or so ago
I might have had a peek:
But Doris hasn't weathered well:
She's eighty-four next week.

Watching Doris bump and grind
Could not have been much grimmer.
Things then went from bad to worse.
She toppled off her Zimmer.

She struggled back upon her feet;
And several minutes later.
She put her teeth back in and said:
I must dominate her!

Now, if you knew our Doris;
You'd know just why I spluttered.
I'd spent two months in traction
For the last complaint I'd suffered.

She stood there nude—naked like,
Bent forward just a bit…
I thought "What the hell"—then stumbled
And stepped on her left tit.

Doris screamed. Her teeth shot out;
My God what had I done?
She moaned and groaned, then shouted out:
"Step on the other one!"

Well readers I can't tell no more;
Of what occurred that day.
Suffice to say my jet-black hair
Turned fifty shades of grey.

SOME TIPS FROM AN OLD MAN

When you see an attractive woman.

No matter how beautiful she is. No matter how sexy she is. No matter how seductive she looks. Even if she has a lovely figure…

Erm.

I've completely forgotten where I am going with this.

Sorry for wasting your time.

LAUGHTER ON THE LINKS

The next and final few pages are devoted exclusively to golf stories but some may also appeal to a non- golfer's sense of humour.

HEAVENLY GOLF

All golfers when they die would love to enjoy everlasting golf in heaven. After all there are some beautiful courses up there, including the exclusive and prestigious Paradise Links Club which boasts among its members both St Peter and Jesus who used to play together regularly, but not any more.

This follows an incident on the long par three 17th when, with their scores level, Jesus sliced his shot way out of bounds. However, it struck a rock, bounced into a pond and was picked up by a frog, which was then grabbed by a hawk which flew over the green with the frog in its beak. The frog croaked and dropped the ball which landed in the hole.

"Are we gonna play golf?" said Peter, "Or you just gonna fuck around?"

A WIFE'S SACRIFICE

A couple were having dinner one evening when the husband reached across the table, held his wife's hand and said, "Beth, soon we will have been married 30 years. I think we have reached the time in our relationship where we can be honest with each other. Tell me, in all of those years of marriage, have you ever been unfaithful to me?"

Beth replied, "Well, Charles, I have to be honest with you. Yes, I have been unfaithful to you three times, but always for a good reason."

Charles was hurt by this confession but curious nonetheless. "Can you please explain to me what those 'good reasons' were?"

"The very first time," said Beth, "was shortly after we were married and we were about to lose our little house because we couldn't pay the mortgage. Do you remember one evening I went to see the bank manager and the next day we received a letter to say that our loan had been extended?"

"Okay," said Charles. "Yes, you saved our home. What about the second time?"

"Remember when you were sick but we didn't have the money to pay for your heart surgery?" Beth said. "And remember I went to see the surgeon one night, after which he did the operation for free?"

"You did that to save my life," said Charles. "Of course I forgive you for that. What about the third time?"

"All right," said Beth. "Are you ready for this?"

Charles nodded.

"So," said Beth, "do you remember when you ran for president of the golf club and you needed 73 more votes?"

THE CHAMPION

"Why," Ted's exasperated wife used to say to him, "do you keep on playing golf when, clearly, you are useless?"

She had listened every week for twenty years to detailed descriptions of his day on the links. The missed putts, sliced drives, how many shots it would take him to get out of bunkers—and how unlucky he had been to find his ball in there in the first place. Thousands of reasons why he had never been even near to winning.

Then one day it all happened for Ted. His drives were more or less straight. His ball never found the bunkers and he sunk some decent putts. He played well. Well enough in fact to win a medal.

So thrilled with his victory in fact, that he insisted on buying everyone drinks all night.

It was late when he eventually arrived home. The house was in darkness and his wife had obviously escaped to bed.

So he didn't switch on the lights, took off his shoes and crept quietly into bed beside his wife who he could sense was not asleep.

He whispered into her ear. "How would you like to make love to a champion golfer?"

"OK," she said. "But you'd better be quick. Ted could be back any minute."

ST ANDREWS

Standing on the first tee at St Andrews addressing the ball, I noticed the club secretary walking down from the clubhouse. He stopped beside the tee box and as I was preparing to take my shot, he coughed and interrupted my concentration. I aborted my attempt to play the ball.

I settled down to address the ball once more and was again interrupted by the club secretary, this time loudly muttering something about etiquette and visitors.

I tried to ignore the remarks and, for a third time, attempted to play my shot.

"It's disgraceful" said the secretary to his friend. Again I was obliged to abort my shot.

I turned round exasperated and said "Have you got a problem mate?"

"Your ball is two yards in front of the tee markers" was the secretary's critical remark.

"Yes. I know" I replied. "Will you now shut up while I play my second bloody shot."

THERAPY

Before waiting for a men's four ball to clear the fairway, a woman golfer played her shot and her ball headed at pace towards one of the men who collapsed to the ground in agony with his hands clasped together at his groin.

The woman rushed to him and apologised profusely, suggesting that she may be able to help since she was a physiotherapist. "I know how to relieve the pain if you will allow me," she told him.

"No, I'll be alright," he said, but he was obviously in pain, lying in the foetal position still clasping his hands at his groin.

At her insistence however, he finally allowed the woman to help.

She gently took his hands away and laid them at his sides, loosened his pants, put her hand inside and skilfully administered a gentle massage for several minutes.

"Now, how does that feel?" she asked.

He replied, "It feels wonderful but I still think my thumb might be broken."

BILL & HARRY

I visited my old golf club recently and was surprised to find that two of the old members who had played together four times a week for many years, no longer did so.

I asked Bill why, because for many years they were inseparable.

"Well," said Bill, "would you want to play with someone who shoots a six and puts himself down for a four on the card?"

"I suppose not," I replied.

"And," continued Bill, "would you want to play with someone who picks up his marker on the green and replaces his ball several inches closer to the hole?"

"No, not really," I replied.

"And would you want to play with someone who nudges his ball with his foot to get a better lie in the rough?" asked Bill.

"Oh, definitely not," I said.

"Would you want to play with someone who carries a duplicate ball in his pocket so he can drop it near to where he thinks his lost ball is?" Bill continued.

"Never!" I replied.

"Well" said Bill, "Neither would Harry."

BILL'S BOAST

"When I was your age, with a lofted club, I could hit a ball right over that tree," said Bill to a young golfer preparing to tee off.

So the young lad gave it everything he had but his ball hit the tree and bounced into the rough.

"Wow," said the young lad, "you must have been some striker of the ball to get over that."

"Not really," said Bill. "It was only a sapling then."

GOLFER'S HANDBOOK

Here are some extracts from a booklet being compiled, with some handy tips for newcomers to the game and some terms to describe the various repertoire of shots. Highlights include:

Chapter 1. How to properly line up your fourth putt.

Chapter 2. How to hit a Maxfli from the rough when you've just hit a Titleist from the tee.

Chapter 3. How to add further distance to your shank.

Chapter 4. Ten excuses for drinking beer before 9am.

Chapter 5. How to find that ball that everyone else saw go into the water.

Chapter 6. How to relax when you are hitting 3 off the tee.

Chapter 7. How to relax when hitting 5 off the tee.

Chapter 8. How to do this with the following four ball waiting behind you on the tee with hands on hips.

...and a variety of shot descriptions:

A Paris Hilton: An expensive hole.

A Diego Maradonna: A nasty 5-footer.

A Salman Rushdie: An impossible read.

A Rock Hudson: Thought it was straight, but it wasn't.

A Yasser Arafat: An ugly lie in the sand.

A Cuban: Needs one more revolution.

A Gerry Adams: Playing a provisional.

A Condom: A safe shot but not much satisfaction.

A Stevie Wonder: Didn't see it.

A Rodney King: Over clubbed.

An O J Simpson: Got away with it.

A Sister in law's Knickers: Out of bounds but I'll play it anyway.

An Adolf Hitler: 2 shots in the bunker.

A Princess Grace: Should have taken a driver.

A Princess Di: Shouldn't have taken a driver.

Beware u golfers!

The bee sting

A young woman had been taking golf lessons.

She had just started playing her first round of golf when she suffered a bee sting.

Her pain was so intense that she decided to return to the clubhouse for help and to complain.

Her golf pro Graham saw her come into the clubhouse and asked, 'Why are you back in so early? What's wrong?'

'I was stung by a bee,' she said.

'Where?' he asked.

'Between the first and second hole,' she replied.

He nodded knowingly and said, 'Then your feet were too far apart.'

CLUCK CLUCK

A golfer sliced his ball into an adjoining chicken farm and it killed one of the hens.

He asked the farmer if he could replace it.

"It depends," said the farmer. "How many eggs a week can you lay?"

A GOLF BALL is like an egg.

It is usually white.

You buy them by the dozen.

…. and a week later you probably have to buy more.

…and finally, AN ODE TO THE DIMPLED BALL

In my hand I hold a ball
Dimpled, white and rather small
Oh how benign it does appear
This harmless looking little sphere.

By its size no one could guess
What awesome power it does possess
But since I fell beneath its spell
I've wandered through the fires of Hell

My life has not been quite the same
Since I chose to play this stupid game
My mind's consumed for hours on end
A fortune it has made me spend

It's made me yell and curse and cry
To hate myself and want to die
It promises me a thing called par
If I can hit it straight and far

To master such a tiny ball
Should surely not be hard at all
But my desires the ball refuses
And does exactly what it chooses

It hooks and slices, dribbles and dies
It can disappear before my very eyes
And often on a truculent whim
Will hit a tree or take a swim

With miles of grass on which to land
It finds a tiny patch of sand
I would offer up my heart and soul
For it to find its elusive hole

It makes me whimper like a pup
And swear that I will give it up
And take to drink to ease my sorrow
But knows too well I'll be back tomorrow.

ENJOYED IT?

Rate it and review it.

FOOTNOTE

The royalties from this book will be paid into my Charities Aid Foundation Account out of which the following donations will be made:

To Royal charities in recognition of the dignified acceptance by the Royals of the often unkind fun made of them.

To Irish charities for the good-natured manner in which the Irish accept and are happy to smile at "Paddy" jokes.

To Religious charities, to demonstrate that, whilst poking fun at some of their practises, I recognise and respect that, in a free society, they have a right to hold and expound their beliefs JUST LIKE THE REST OF US.

Derrick Arnott
December 2019

PS. If you have an amusing, interesting or mischievous quip, rant, tale, graphic or joke which is worthy of inclusion in a second edition, please send it by email to <u>inboxdez@yahoo.co.uk.</u>